THE ART OF

Also by Sheila Bridge

The Art of Imperfect Parenting

The Art of Plate Spinning

Being a Mother with a Crowded Lifestyle

Sheila Bridge

Hodder & Stoughton
LONDON SYDNEY AUCKLAND

Copyright © Sheila Bridge 1996

First published in Great Britain 1996

The right of Sheila Bridge to be identified as the Author of
the Work has been asserted by her in accordance with the
Copyright, Designs and Patents Act 1988.

10 9 8 7 6 5 4 3 2 1

All rights reserved. No part of this publication may be
reproduced, stored in a retrieval system, or transmitted,
in any form or by any means without the prior written permission
of the publisher, nor be otherwise circulated in any form of binding
or cover other than that in which it is published and without a
similar condition being imposed on the subsequent purchaser.

British Library Cataloguing in Publication Data
A record for this book is available from the British Library

ISBN 0 340 66185 2

Printed and bound in Great Britain by
Cox & Wyman, Reading, Berks

Hodder and Stoughton Ltd
A Division of Hodder Headline PLC
338 Euston Road
London NW1 3BH

Contents

Foreword

This book scratches where I itch. It tells the true story.

For years I wondered whether there was such a thing as the 'new Christian woman' – the equivalent of society's 'new man', she who had it all: a husband, home, children, career, social life, leisure, dog, cat, budgie and the church, though not necessarily in that order. Could I be the competent career woman with a well-groomed image, a dutiful wife with an hour-glass figure, a loving mother with well-behaved children, and a tireless church-worker with a disciplined spiritual life?

The answer, I discovered, and I'm so glad we have Sheila Bridge to say it, is a resounding no!

The problem was that I was completely taken in by those glitzy advertising images. First, there's a blissful early motherhood, when I thought I would live and move in a permanent soft-focused haze of loving contentment, with nothing to do but sit and gaze in uninterrupted adoration at the tranquil little bundle at my breast. The truth was a combination of utter exhaustion and mental atrophy, complicated by a large dose of helpless inadequacy. Oh, and sore breasts. They never tell you about that, or about colic, interrupted nights, and endless washing.

Then, with children safely deposited in the local primary school, there's the woman returner, complete with Dior suit, power briefcase and flick-through-the-fingers hair-do, who comes home to an immaculate gingerbread house, food bubbling merrily on the stove, and children tucked up happily, waiting for that bedtime story. When Central TV asked me to join them as a full-time researcher once both my children were at school, it was an offer I couldn't refuse. I was fortunate, married to a clergyman who could take two hours off at 3.30 before doing an evening shift. But the church had to do without me, my cooking skills gave up on me, and so did many of my friends. And my tights were always laddered. They don't tell you about that either.

Ah but now I have teenagers, old enough to take care of themselves, or so I was led to believe. Now I'm supposed to play the Persil Mum, whose children shine with a dazzling outer (and inner?) purity, or the Bisto Mum, whose family is so well fed, they never fight, so radiantly healthy, she can sit back satisfied, knowing she has given them all they will ever need to ensure a halcyon future. No, this is the era of filthy boots lined up in the kitchen, theirs and their enormous friends', of a mysteriously and permanently empty freezer, of going to work with half-closed lids because you sat up half the night, analysing their romantic problems, or just waiting for them to come in. This is when gravity does awful things to your body. They do tell you about that. The suggestions are expensive and time-consuming.

All the stages have been wonderful – if utterly exhausting. They would have been even more enjoyable if I had had this invaluable book to hand – and Sheila Bridge to help me see that behaving like a demented hamster on a wheel was a common experience.

All power to her elbow for her taking the time and trouble to research her subject so carefully, for when women begin to pool their ideas, it makes life that little bit easier. This is a subject we should have been discussing years ago. Sheila Bridge has provided us with an invaluable opportunity now. I, for one, would be very sad if we missed it.

Michele Guinness

Introduction

It used to be fashionable to describe people in terms of neat mnemonics. Speaking personally, I never quite made it as a Yuppie (a 'young, upwardly mobile person') but I did spend some time as a Dinky (a 'double income, no kids yet' couple), before I became a Triffid, which sounds far less attractive ('two recent infants, finances firmly in decline'). However, now that my children are not quite such recent arrivals, now that all sorts of possibilities are opening up for me to do all sorts of things, including shoring up the family's income, I find my life has become too complicated to be neatly summed up by a set of initials.

In spite of my inner rebellion against the notion that I can be defined by what I do, I have to accept the fact that explaining what I do is one of the simplest ways people can begin to understand me. My personal list of roles and accomplishments includes being a wife, a parent, a part-time employee, a live-in domestic (in my own home, thankfully), a toddler group leader, a social secretary, an author, a counsellor, a provider of provisions, a correspondent, a gardener and a zoo-keeper (two guinea-pigs hardly constitute a zoo, but it can feel that way). Your personal profile may well be even more varied so is there a term that we can use to neatly define ourselves? What *are* we? In a word . . . exhausted! (that's an adjective, I've had it with mnemonics, silly idea, impossibly spelt!).

Of all the books we've ever had out from the children's library, there is one I especially enjoyed. It was a picture book called *Isn't She Clever.*[1] In it the attention of two young children is drawn to all the things their mother does for them. Each of her activities is then compared to its professional equivalent so that by the end of the book the children realise that their mother is 'a cook, a gardener, a nurse, a taxi-driver, a hair-dresser, a zoo-keeper, a teacher, a decorator, a dress-maker, and a window-cleaner'. The book closes with the rhetorical question 'Isn't she clever?' to which I could never resist a resounding reply in the affirmative.

It's reassuring to find a book that paints such a comprehensive picture of a mother's vocation and raises it to the professional status it deserves. However, several facets of an 'average' mother's life have been overlooked in this particular book: first, the ironing; second, the cleaning. The omission of these two boring obligations might be put down to a reluctance to suggests that these tasks should be seen as 'female' duties. Quite right too ... in theory. In reality, sadly not so. Most of us females still do the lion's share (to use an ironically masculine metaphor) of the 'chores'. This is not an opinion but a well-researched statistical fact. The British Social Attitudes Report 1984 found that in married and cohabiting partnership the chores (washing, ironing, meal preparation, cleaning, shopping, looking after sick children and washing-up) were overwhelmingly done by the woman.

The third omission in my children's story-book was far more glaring: the mother in that story had no paid employment outside the home. No matter what your views on working mothers, according to a recent newspaper survey 'almost one in three of the total labour force are women with family responsibilities'.[2] It is simply unrealistic to overlook the fact that many women's lives also feature a bracing dash of paid employment outside the home.

In 1990 another report revealed that 90 per cent of the British population felt that women had a right to work whatever their family situation.[3] There is a certain ironic ambiguity about this attitude because the underlying expectation is that women should be able to work assuming they are still able to attend to all the needs of the household. Why is it that the newspaper survey didn't bother to find out how many men in the labour force have family responsibilities? Clearly because these responsibilities are not expected to affect a man's labour in the way that they affect a woman's.

Whatever you feel about society's unfair expectation that women should shoulder both work and home, it is the most likely explanation for the fact that 80 per cent of the women who do take up 'paid employment' do so part-time, by choice.[4] I do not intend getting into a heavy debate about whether this situation is 'right' or 'wrong', but simply to recognise that it is so and to consider the way that this reality impacts on women's lives.

The statistic about part-time work always makes me wince because most women I know work 'full-time'; they just don't get paid for that part of their labours that are in the home or with children. So, because paid labour is not the only activity that makes demands on our time, we end up as part-time employees, part-time parents, part-time partners, part-time volunteers at church or school . . . in fact if you add up all the parts of your life, it can sometimes feel as if you are living three and a half lives in the space where one ought to be.

The focus of this book is on busy parents, mothers in particular. That doesn't mean to imply that people without children are not busy. On the contrary, they are just as likely to fulfil a multitude of roles. The difference for parents is that the list of possible activities and responsibilities multiplies to such an extent it can be hard to see 'the wood for the trees'. It is possible to lose your sense of direction because you lose that sense of doing anything 'full-time' or whole-heartedly. Your first awareness of this feeling may have been when you put your baby down for a nap and flew round the house trying to do in half an hour everything that could not be done with twelve pounds of baby in your arms. Or perhaps it came later when it seemed like your chatty toddler's main aim in life was to ensure you never uttered an uninterrupted sentence, nor could you complete a task without at least four diversions from that task.

The sense of exhaustion and confusion that results from being pulled simultaneously in different directions only gets worse as the children get older and your 'options' multiply: will you return to work? Will you hear children read at school? Will you run the PTA? Will you go on the rota for arranging the flowers in church? The possibilities are endless. Meanwhile, you are still the home's resident nutritionalist, the social organiser and everyone's favourite shoulder to cry on . . .

This book is for anyone who has ever felt overstretched and exhausted; anyone who has ever felt the pressure of having so many roles, so many plates spinning in their lives that they feel harrassed and painfully aware that one or two of the plates are crashing more often than they would like, due to lack of time and attention.

It's not going to be a discussion about which plates you ought not to be spinning. It starts with an acceptance of life as it is. In brief, this book aims to tell you, not what you should or shouldn't do, but how to do what you want to do without being 'done in' in the process.

I have written from experience and not just from my own. Almost a hundred women from varying backgrounds have completed a detailed questionnaire about their lives, passing on to me, not just a picture of where they are at in life but also an abundance of practical suggestions: ways in which they have made life run as smoothly and efficiently as possible. These ideas have been collated at the end of each appropriate chapter, forming a sort of at-a-glance, 'here's-one-that-worked-for-me' suggestion list. I am very grateful for all their help and resourcefulness.

It simply remains to say that there is no implied order of importance in the way the chapters have been arranged. Children do not take priority over their husbands nor homemaking over service for God, just because they are discussed in that order. You are the only one who can determine, before God, your own order of priorities. Our lives do make simultaneous contact with most of the following subjects: motherhood, homemaking, paid labour, Christian/voluntary service, and relationships but none of these come at us in the neatly wrapped compartments that these chapter distinctions seem to suggest. Even though it is impossible to impose such divisions on life, these headings are intended as helpful guides; allowing you to assess where you are, how you got there and where you'd like to be, not unlike an exercise in map-reading. So between the setting off point of Chapter 1 and the summing up in Chapter 9, please feel free to shuffle the subjects around and read them in whatever order best reflects your own uniquely crowded life.

Chapter 1

I Do Everything . . . Part-Time

'What do you do?'

Such an innocent little question! So often employed early on in any new relationship. For some of us it is so fiendishly difficult to answer.

If the question is actually a none-too-subtle attempt to get an easy handle on who I am, I have to swallow hard on my irritation. Even if the question conveys genuine interest I still face a dilemma and usually waste several seconds surveying my options: how much time have they got? How interested are they?

Shall I say, 'I'm a housewife'? Not the best opening line for stimulating conversation, nor is it entirely true. If my house could speak it would disown me.

Shall I say, 'I'm a mother'? This will lead the conversation past the exchange of irrelevant information to a full stop and neither of us will retain anything we have heard about the names and ages of our respective offspring.

Shall I say, 'I'm David's wife. He's the blah, blah, blah, of blah blah'? Certainly not! As much as I love and respect him, I am not defined by his reflected glory!

This leaves me with the two options my interrogator had in mind. Either 'I work for,' or 'I am a,'. Coward that I am, I usually bow to expectations and opt for 'I am a writer' but only if I feel up to the usual flood of remarks and questions that come prefixed by the phrase, 'How interesting'. Seeing as writing only takes up eight to nine hours a week, this answer still doesn't really convey the whole picture of what I do. So when I'm feeling reclusive I offer 'I run a Parent and Toddler group' because this is another guaranteed conversation stopper, unless the person to whom you are speaking also happens to run one. In which case a warmly receptive, creative and understanding conversation is likely to ensue. (Three cheers for toddler group leaders everywhere!)

One of these days I will eventually pluck up the courage to give the only truly honest answer there is to the casual enquiry, 'What do you *do*?'

'I breathe.'

Breathing is the only activity I *do* full-time. When I cease to breathe all my many and various activities will come to a sudden and permanent stop. These activities do not define me, they are not me, they are simply the way I choose to spend my time.

The urge to justify our existence in terms of what we do seems to be one to which the whole human race falls prey. Women, mothers in particular, have the added frustration that, because their lives are so varied and changeable their life cannot be so easily defined. Thus, it is easier for them to feel insecure and uncertain about who they are. They might feel that life is like making a blanket of different coloured crochet squares. Each little part is attractive in itself but disjointed and 'bitty' unless it is part of a meaningful whole. For many of us, the biggest challenge in life is its sheer 'busyness'; life is such an unrelenting rush of activity we rarely get the time to 'sew' all the various parts together. We don't have time to make sense of our experience.

I have had days when the list of things to do is so long and complicated I often feel like adding a final reminder at the end of the list: 'Breathe!' Hardly any wonder then, that breathlessness is often linked to anxiety and deep breathing so often recommended as a calming cure. It seems more like a call to simply 'be' instead of 'do'.

The Effect of 'Busyness'

When you feel 'done-in' by all the things there are to do, all
the enjoyment goes out of life. Recently our family passed
through a particularly busy phase: every week-end had more
crammed into it than should have been possible; our normal
load of responsibilities seemed to be trebling in weight; at
least three major decisions were playing on our minds and
refusing to be quickly settled; on top of all this we were
taking it in turns to be ill. Several weeks of life lived in such
a way resulted in a change of outlook: people who we
normally enjoyed seeing suddenly seemed 'demanding'; the
phone became an enemy not merely a tool; and I began to
weigh up every activity to determine its 'exhaustion' rather
than its 'enjoyment' factor.

'How did we get into this situation?' was the question we
asked ourselves. We never meant for life to get so out of
control. It wasn't only out of control, we'd also stopped
having fun. We just felt weary all the time and it wasn't
simply due to being ill. Even being ill was, in part, a reaction
to the lifestyle we'd adopted. With the benefit of hindsight
and once we were a little way past this busy period, it
dawned on me why we had got in such a mess. We had
stopped being 'pro-active' and started being 'reactive'.
Instead of being in charge of what we needed/wanted to do,
we had just said 'yes' to everything that had come along;
hence the diary bulging with social engagements and the
ever-lengthening list of responsibilities.

To be pro-active means to exercise your freedom of choice
with appropriate assertiveness and direct your life according
to your own needs, desires and hopes without being unduly
concerned or swayed by other people's opinions and expectations. If you are a Christian, then being pro-active means
living your life under God's direction, according to his
unique plan for your life.

To be reactive means to go through life having your

choices and options decided for you by the expectations or needs of your immediate family/community/friends/culture (delete as appropriate). Instead of deciding in advance what it is that you want to do (or what it is that God wants you to do), you react to people's opinions, to sermons, to inner feelings of false guilt, people's expectations, circumstances. The list goes on.

Clearly there is a degree to which we cannot help reacting to life's events, and the opinions of loved ones deserve to be heard lest we become arrogant. Reacting appropriately to a rebuke or an unforseen circumstance is often part of being responsive to God. But if the whole tenor of our life becomes reactive instead of pro-active then we have handed over the controls of our lives into the hands of those around us or into the circumstances that befall us.

God calls us to be pro-active. He calls us to be in responsible charge of our own lives. 'Be very careful, then, how you live ... making the most of every opportunity' (Eph. 5:16, 17). We are all called to the same vocation – to love God and to love others. Individually we each have to work out how this vocation will be expressed in our lives; bearing in mind that God's same call on the lives of others may well have a very different expression. They will not always order their lives in the same way that we order ours but that does not mean that one of us is right and the other is wrong.

Why Me?

Why is it that parents, in particular, run the risk of becoming reactive? People without children can be pro-actively busy, but parents tend to be more reactively busy. That is to say that all our time and energy is taken up with events and circumstances over which we have no choice. Certainly, at the outset of parenthood we had a choice: whether or not to have children. But once that choice was made (and some of us got more than we bargained for) all sorts of consequent tasks (feeding, clothing, educating, and loving said offspring) are matters about which we have no choice. Moreover, these tasks are vast consumers of time, energy and resources.

The early days of your career in motherhood was by its very nature reactive. Babies are fed on demand, nappies are changed as required. In fact, at this stage, life runs best if you do 'go with the flow' of your small tyrant's needs.

The danger is that you become locked into a reactive pattern of responding. If this happens your life will be shaped as a result of reacting to your husband's needs, reacting to your children's needs, reacting to the needs of the household to be kept at a minimum level of untidiness. 'What's wrong with that?' you might say. 'These are all very biblical things to do.' And so they are, I agree, but it is surely better to embrace them out of positive choice rather than attend to them simply because they need attending to. At the end of the day, the decade, or at the end of your life you might find you never really got round to doing what you really wanted to do or maybe even to what God was calling you to do because all your time was taken up with things that were simply there to be done. In spite of how things look at the start of parenthood, you do still have a choice over what priority you will give to all the tasks that demand your attention.

Many women find themselves locked into a reactive situation. Living pro-actively can seem like an impossible dream when such a big part of your life is taken up with things that simply *have* to be done. Is it possible to live pro-actively? If so, how can we do it? Are discipline, order and organisation the secrets of a pro-active life? Surely good organisation, combined with a heavy dose of self-discipline is the key to ordering our lives successfully?

Well, maybe these things have their place but they also have their drawbacks. As someone who has lived life dictated by my own lists and lists of lists, I hesitate to recommend them as essential for everyone. Some people like to have a structured and ordered world but other people thrive in an unpredictable world. They are flexible people, spontaneous and so laid-back they are almost horizontal. Needless to say they drive us 'control freaks' round the bend. However, I have learnt a lot from them, too much to wish to dictate to anyone that they must follow a set system for organising their life. I reached a point where I realised that my organisational tools – my diary, my wall-planner, my work goals, my exercise goals, my household goals – were no longer serving me as tools, they were controlling me as tyrants.

Diaries can have drawbacks. They ought to come with health warnings attached. A friend of mine preferred to write all her appointments on her kitchen wall. Not directly, you understand, she did put up a wall-planner first. She did this because à la 'Shirley Valentine' she liked the idea of conversing with her wall. However, she quickly discovered the main disadvantage of this system: walls are not portable. So she invested in a diary but continued to refer to it as her 'wall', a term which I think conveys an appropriate notion of heaviness.

We sometimes assume that just because it is in the diary, we have to do it. This isn't in fact the case. Another friend told me that she wrote the word 'Freedom' in her diary against a certain time slot. A casual glance at time blocked off in this way might have led to all sorts of adventures! In fact, it referred to a Bible study she was meant to be attending.

Everyone in our family who can write anything beyond their name, has a diary. Our daughter is six and has just been given (to her great delight) her first 'Funfax'. She is a highly structured and tidy individual. It's not hard to see who she has modelled herself on. But as I see my reflection in her methodical lifestyle I realise some of the pitfalls for characters like us. At six Emma is just beginning to be aware of the fact that the world is a big bad place, friends don't always stay friends, teachers sometimes misunderstand you, and sometimes dreams don't come true. Whenever life is giving her a hard time out there, I can observe her almost perceptively tightening her grip on her own small world: her room is immaculate, boys are banned, lists of rules go up on the door and special events are planned down to the choice of hair-slide.

'I'm in Charge around Here'

For my daughter this controlling behaviour is understandable and completely normal but it speaks volumes to me of my own attitude towards routine and organisation. By becoming 'more organised' am I trying to grab life by the throat and force things to go my way? How then do I cope when they don't? Do I fall apart when the house is disorderly, the deadlines unmet or my social engagements rearranged? Am I trying to control my world and protect my little empire? If so, techniques and systems for time management will certainly help me. On the other hand if I've handed the control of my life over to God, then my organisational style must remain as a mere tool to help me live more calmly and effectively.

I've read books on how to use your time wisely that suggest cleaning rotas and washing-up charts. Other books have urged me to have annual goals, monthly goals, weekly goals and daily goals. By the time the writer was pressing me on towards hourly goals I felt as if a large mallet was pounding me down into a particularly narrow hole in the ground. The only suitable epitaph for being so buried alive being a notice saying 'Pretty Tight Schedule – No People Allowed'. People, especially the smaller variety, are notorious disrupters of schedules, so if we want to have time to hold people we must learn to hold our schedules lightly.

The way that people run their lives often reveals what they believe life is for. Is it to be enjoyed? Or is it to be put to good use? Many of us have laboured so long and hard

under the Protestant work ethic, believing that every part of
our life ought to have some useful purpose, that we have
forgotten that life is meant to be enjoyed. The catechism
says that our purpose is to know God and to enjoy him
forever. Jesus said he had come that we might have 'abun-
dant life' but some of us work, eat, and even relax in such a
way that you'd think life is an endurance test, not an
enjoyment. If we really are enjoying ourselves then maybe
we are doing something wrong and God is going to notice
his oversight at any moment and put us to some hard task.
This faulty idea about God being a kind of divine policeman
can sometimes be the reason why someone is pushed into
overdrive. Even my own enthusiasm for diaries may have
been prompted by this kind of idea. I clearly remember the
headmaster of my junior school taking an assembly on the
virtue of good record-keeping. He greatly impressed me by
saying how useful his own diary had been when he had been
interviewed by the police. I was so overawed by this
efficiency that, in my childish innocence, it didn't occur to
me to wonder why he had been questioned by the police in
the first place. Who knows, perhaps ever since, my enthusiasm for diaries and lists has been fuelled by some inner
subconscious fear that I might, at any moment, be required
to give an account of my movements to a member of the
local constabulary.

For all I've said about the pitfalls of these organisational
tools and systems, there's no doubt in my mind that routine
is a valuable back-drop to my life. A structured lifestyle and
helpful policies free me up from having to think about life's
more mundane tasks. I don't want to save a space in my
mind or in my week in order to be flexible and open about
when and where I shop. If I know it is every other Wednesday afternoon at a certain store, then that's several tedious
decisions taken at a stroke. But life is not all about routines
and strategies, I have come to accept the need to be flexible
and have found that it is healthy to be able to step outside
the routines from time to time.

The Secret of Plate Spinning

We will come back again and again to consider the helpful routines and strategies that make our lives run smoother as we look at each aspect of our lives. However, I hope that I've made it clear at the outset that these are only the practical tools towards a good plate-spinning technique. So what, then, is the secret of successful plate spinning? I'd like to suggest that the secret lies in being able to answer two questions: 'How do I want to live my life?' and 'What kind of person am I?'

If I ask myself the first question 'How do I want to live my life?' the answer I give is more about the *way* I do what I do, rather than the *what* of what I do. 'How shall I live?' does not answer the type of dilemmas such as 'Shall I work?', 'Will I volunteer for x, y or z?' or 'Which chores shall I do when?' but it's got rather more to do with the quality of my life, however it is filled. This is what I came up with:

I want to be productively busy, but not harassed.
I want to be creatively occupied, but not overstretched.
I want to be able to love my family and build friendships.
I want my world to be reasonably well ordered.
I want to be able to live in such a way that I can give each task, each moment my full time and attention.
I want to be able to read bedtime stories to my kids without having the moment spoilt by the pressure building up in my mind about all the other things I have yet to do that evening.
I want to enjoy greeting them out from school by slowing down to their pace and laying aside my own preoccupations.
When I'm working I want to work whole-heartedly.
When I'm relaxing I want to relax completely.
When I'm with people I love or people who hurt I want

to be fully 'with them', not with half my mind on other things.

In short, I want to be fruitfully engaged with the world on the outside but quiet on the inside.

Is this description achievable or is it a dream? I believe it is possible and preferable to be able to live life in this way, walking quietly from one moment to the next. It is so far removed from the frenetic analogy of our lives as an exercise in plate spinning that it sounds more like a ballet, but I know which I'd prefer.

What I need in order to live calmly and peacefully is something more than a scheme or a strategy. I don't need a more rigorous schedule that simply tells me *what* to do. I have little trouble knowing what to do. What I need is a way of living that tells me *how* to do it, without being 'done-in' by it all.

It is unrealistic to keep going when we are busy by telling ourselves that 'a quieter time is coming, the children will become less demanding, life will get easier'. Even if this were true, it doesn't help us much in the here and now when we feel overloaded. Our children are growing up fast. If I don't stop and enjoy having a six-year-old now, I won't have one, because in a few months, she'll be seven.

Redeem the time, 'carpe diem' goes the motto. In other words, make sure you are doing now the things you most want to do. This isn't meant to drive us into greater and greater activity, only to make us stop and consider, 'Is the way I am living now, regardless of what I am doing, the way I really want to be living?' Given the constraints of my circumstances, am I being reactive or pro-active?

Even though we may have a pro-active approach to life, life does not always co-operate with us. We have to be realistic about the circumstances that we are in and start with a realistic acceptance of life as it is. Your life is probably busy. It is unlikely to get any less busy. This being true, the only way forward is to find a way of living it that prevents us from being shipwrecked. I find a sailing analogy very helpful. If you imagine your life as a sailing trip (ghastly thought for some of us I know, but bear with me) then the boat represents your life. You are basically 'sound' and seaworthy but you leak a bit and your navigational equipment is not totally reliable. Add to this the fact that the world in which you move is an ocean of possibilities and hazards and you can start to see why life is not always 'plain sailing'. If you are going to sail successfully then it pays you to know 'What are the main hazards out there?', 'What is my little boat capable of?' and 'Where I am going?'

A crowded lifestyle can potentially be productive, enjoyable and fulfilling but what are the hazards we face? First of all, there are the currents. Other people's expectations can be an overwhelming current that can send us crashing on to the rocks of over-commitment. Then there is the overwhelming tide of legitimate demands from our offspring that can leave our marriage or friendships crashing on the rock of neglect or undernourishment. We can't change these hazards. They will always be there, but if we know ourselves well and, perhaps more importantly, if we have a skilful pilot on board we can successfully navigate around them.

Second, we have to know our own vessel and its capabilities. This is similar to the question, 'What type of person am I?' If I have a temperament that thrives in an ordered and structured environment, then certain crowded lifestyles could be disorientating and frustrating for me. If on top of this I am an introvert, that is I am fuelled by time spent alone, then any lifestyle that is full of people will quickly drain me, unless sufficient time is allowed for refuelling.

Drawing Your Own Map

Finally, 'Where are you going?' When you are on any journey, it can be a useful exercise to stop and look around you to determine exactly where you are. You need at some time to pull over and pull out the map. Continuing onwards whilst uncertain of your direction can be a very dangerous thing to do. So before we leave this chapter, the starting point for our journey, I recommend a short exercise. It is adapted from time-management exercises but try to think of it as a way of drawing your own unique map.

There are various ways to do this exercise, but this is the way I have found most helpful. You'll need at least half an hour of peace and quiet and a fairly clear head. First of all, write down the five things you most want to do. These should be things that are the ongoing achievements of daily life, not the one-offs such as 'climb Everest' that would require you to step outside of your daily life. Here are some suggestions to get you thinking: 'spend time shaping my children', 'use my talents creatively', 'bring others to faith', 'spend more time with my partner', 'be successful in my career', 'grow a lovely garden'.

Next, fill in the time chart printed near here or a photocopy of it if you don't want to leave a week in your life lying around. Be honest. Put what you actually did, not what you intended to do. Don't wait for a 'good week' to do this exercise. Don't say, 'Ah, yes but last week was different.' Unless you were away on holiday or experienced a major life event such as a marriage, birth or death, then the chances are that last week was about as 'different' as next week will be. There is no such thing as a 'normal' week. I think it was Mark Twain who said, 'Life is just one darn thing after another.'

When you have filled in the chart, go back to your list of goals and add up the number of hours you spent doing the thing you most want to do. Then stand back and make an assessment. How are you doing? Are you reaching any or all of your goals? Which one is getting the least time and why? Is that reasonable, given the stage of life you are at? Is there anything you can do to change the situation?

Finally, for the purpose of mapping your way through this book, you might like to return to your time chart and add

Hours	Sunday	Monday	Tuesday	Wednesday	Thursday	Friday	Saturday
12–5 a.m.							
5–6 a.m.							
6–7 a.m.							
7–8 a.m.							
8–9 a.m.							
9–10 a.m.							
10–11 a.m.							
11–12 a.m.							
12–1 p.m.							
1–2 p.m.							

Hours	Sunday	Monday	Tuesday	Wednesday	Thursday	Friday	Saturday
2–3 p.m.							
3–4 p.m.							
4–5 p.m.							
5–6 p.m.							
6–7 p.m.							
7–8 p.m.							
8–9 p.m.							
9–10 p.m.							
10–11 p.m.							
11–12 p.m.							

up the amount of time you spent on the following headings: mothering, paid employment, homemaking, church work, relationships, and time spent nourishing your spiritual life. Which aspect of your life is getting the most time and attention and is this how you want it to be?

'Life's Rich Tapestry'?

One of my mother's favourite devotional poems begins 'My life is but a weaving, between my Lord and I'. This rather suggests that life is a cosy activity worked out beside an intimate fireplace. 'Life's rich tapestry' is a phrase that denotes much the same idea. By the time you have completed your chart and compared it with your goals you may well feel that your life is as far removed from a quiet fireplace as a storm at sea. Perhaps your small vessel is tossed about by the currents and winds and your most persistent feeling is the seasickness of uncertainty and anxiety, your most persistent fear that of losing direction completely.

It's one thing to sail about aimlessly on a sunny day but quite another to go purposefully in a desired direction when the elements are not co-operating. The presence of a pilot in such a situation would not merely be an asset, it would be an outright necessity.

In just such a way, we each need a pilot, someone at the helm of our lives, a calm presence on the 'bridge'. The best pilot is the one who knows us best because he created us. He is also the one who has a purpose and direction for our lives. He cannot be pinned down to a time or a place, a system or a schedule; he does not 'come aboard' as a helpful crew passenger, nor is he merely a life-saver in storms. When he enters our lives, he comes as the pilot, the captain of our vessel. Or, as he was known to those fishermen disciples, the Master. It is only in relationship with him that we can master the art of ordering our lives and setting our priorities.

Jesus was there in the boat with the disciples on the day when the storm blew up. But the disciples were experienced fishermen. Surely they could handle this crisis? They'd weathered storms before. Even though he was there, they only woke him when they reached the point of fearing for their lives.

Jesus didn't always still storms. When he called to Peter to step out of the boat the waves were choppy and the wind was strong. Peter could 'walk' calmly in the most unlikely of circumstances if he kept his eyes on the Master's power to sustain him. He only sank when he looked instead at all that threatened to engulf him.

So it isn't just the conditions we're in that determine our way of life, though we do well to take these into account. Ultimately, it is the presence of the pilot, the master navigator, that can free us to live the way we were created to live, to be the kind of people we were created to be and to order our lives in a way that reflects a calm trust in the competence of our captain.

Chapter 2

Motherhood: The Shoe Woman Stage

There was an old woman who lived in a shoe,
She had so many children, she didn't know what to do.

You've probably never thought of yourself as a 'shoe woman'. As most illustrations of this nursery rhyme feature an old lady in eighteenth-century dress living in a converted boot with upwards of fifty children, it can seem somewhat removed from your situation especially if you live in a neat 'semi' with your average 2.4 children.

If this phrase doesn't sum up how you perceive yourself at that stage when most of your children are preschool, then it certainly sums up how you may be perceived by others. It was a friend of mine who inspired this title. She had gone with her three children to another friend's house for lunch. The hostess had two children of her own at home, so the total number of kids around the kitchen table was a mere five. While they were chatting a third friend dropped by. Seeing all the children first before he noticed and recognised my friend, he remarked (and it had to be a 'he' didn't it?),

'Oh, it's you! I might have known it would be you with *all* these kids.'

My friend was left speechless but fortunately she recovered her powers of speech and reason by the time she recounted the incident to me.

'He made me feel like a shoe woman!' she said, and a chapter title was born!

Women with small children, buggy-pushers doing the toddler-group trail, can often feel just like that: overlooked, belittled or invisible behind a 'crowd' of small children.

They are not noticed as individuals in their own right. They become just another childminding body in the crèche at church, barely noticeable behind the noisy fidgeting of their offspring. Or they are the awkward ones on any form of public transport, folding buggies and clutching reins. People are far more uncomfortably aware of the spilt drinks, running noses and sticky fingers than they are of the needs of the long-suffering parent in tow. Small children have a way of bearing all before them. A mere two children and a push-chair can fill the pavement and move in an irritatingly erratic way. Observe the effect when the same little group enters a local shop: members of the public move back as if there's been an invasion.

Even when you are not with your small children the association can still affect you. I met people who can make an innocent remark such as, 'Oh, yes, you've got small children' sound like, 'Oh, yes, you've got headlice'!

But if the general public can make us feel like unattractive and irresponsible 'shoe women', then it is also true that we can ourselves feel just like the poor old woman in the nursery rhyme in the sense that we feel overwhelmed. It doesn't take fifty children to make you feel overwhelmed. One particularly whining, demanding or irritating child can do the job just as effectively. More commonly it is the 'two under two' situation that brings us to cracking-up point, although I've always thought that 'three under five' probably deserves its reputation. One lady I know has six. She told me quite truthfully that she loved it best when they were all small. I swallowed hard, smiled weakly at her and felt hugely inadequate.

Let's face it, some mothers do come into their own and thrive at this stage of motherhood. I don't think I was one of them. The period when my children were at home full-time had its high points and advantages. It also had extremely low points that were related to feelings like exhaustion and that sense of near personal extinction that comes over you when all you do is clean, cook and cajole small people into at least a degree of co-operation.

Jobs never get finished at this stage of life. Every task is in fact an interruption of the previous task which interrupted the original activity. Small children tend to dress/eat/wash and walk very slowly ... Their conversation is constant, with a high question content. They ensure your total attention by repeating, 'Mum, Mum, Mum ... Maaaaaaum', until you finally respond. If this fails, then a spilt drink, a swipe at their sibling or a stumbling over the stairs will guarantee your immediate attention.

Their diversionary tactics are renowned. These vary from the life-threatening (climbing out of windows) to the merely interesting ('Look! A spider. Look, Mummy. Look!') to the mind-boggling ('So how old *is* God?') to the downright maddening ('She ate my biscuit so I thumped her'). Added to this their sleep patterns are erratic. They wake dreadfully early and are horribly cheerful about it.

These are huge generalisations I know. Your children may not do, or have done, any of these things but all of us surely understand the frustration of never completing one task before the next one comes along. Even the tasks that are completed are the type that never stay done, like the ironing.

After a mere month of motherhood I was so frustrated by this lack of permanence to all my achievements that I set up my sewing-machine and while my daughter took one, fortunately long, afternoon nap I cut out and sewed up a complete skirt. No piece of dressmaking has ever given me such a sense of achievement.

Coming to terms with this loss of identity or lack of achievement can be very hard for some of us. It can feel as though we have lost our sense of self-worth. When you combine this with the fact that we have probably also lost our figures and a fair degree of our dignity, you can begin to see why such a readjustment is hard. For a long while it can feel as if life is dominated by these small children, we can feel glued to them. This can lead to us feeling that we are defined by our offspring rather than as women in our own right. I think it's important to acknowledge this feeling which is often compounded by society's failure to recognise the value and worth of the role mothers have in looking after small children.

There are a number of ways of dealing with this negative feeling: you could take up sewing in spurts; you could read or study some subject totally unrelated to childhood (if you can keep your eyes open); or you could return to work. As someone who has tried all of these options (not purely because I felt negative about my role as a mother), I would not like to dictate to you which ones would be helpful for you. The 'return to work' option has its own pitfalls (as we'll see in Chapter 5) but whatever you do I urge you not to undervalue your own needs as a person. It may be that, for a season, you are prepared to forego your needs but don't discount them as unimportant. If you are becoming depressed due to a lack of intellectual stimulation or a creative outlet, then it might be worth considering whether a 'happier Mummy part-time' would be better than a 'grumpy full-time Mummy' who feels trapped in her role as a mother.

Society has a picture of what a 'good mother' is or does, and most of us waste a lot of emotional energy trying to match ourselves to these images, and suffer a lot of guilt when we feel we don't make the grade or come up to people's expectations ('Shouldn't he be out of nappies by now?' 'Can't she tell the time yet?'). Instead of trying to be all we feel we are 'expected' to be, we need to learn to say, 'I want to be the best mother that I can be, given my personality and my situation.'

In the end two thoughts helped me. First, I recognised that this was a season of my life, it was not going to last forever. Every season has its fruits and its drawbacks but the only way to live at peace with this season of early motherhood is to give yourself totally to it. I wanted to look back without any regrets that I'd missed any of the experiences and opportunities that this season offered me. Don't take that remark about giving yourself whole-heartedly to the season as precluding any outside interests, hobbies or work. I'm referring more to your attitude than to what you actually do. If you whole-heartedly accept the drawbacks and limitations of life with small children as being transitory then you will be more at peace. Half-heartedness and wishing yourself five years forward leads to resentment, grumbling and missed opportunities. On the other hand, once you've settled in your mind to accept the re-ordered priorities that small children bring then you are free to explore what you can do during this season of life.

It can be a wonderful time for forming new and strongly supportive friendships with other women. It can be a time for exploring new talents you didn't know you had (well, finger-painting could be classed as artwork!). Most of all from a spiritual point of view it can be a time to know yourself loved by God for who you are and not for what you do. If we ourselves can begin to believe how much God loves us for who we are at the outset of parenting, then we have surely learnt the most precious lesson we can possibly pass on to our children.

The second thing that helped me was to view my role 'professionally'. By this I mean giving it, by my attitude, the status I felt it deserved. I refused to see myself as 'just a mum' or 'just a housewife'. I set myself goals, not ridiculously high expectations such as maintaining a tidy house, but achievable goals that made me feel as though I was doing a job and not just passing the time. In the early days it would be things like washing up the breakfast dishes before lunch or getting out of the house once a day. Later on as the children's needs changed my goals would change to things like reading to them once a day. I was very impressed by the phrase, 'If you aim at nothing, then that's what you'll probably hit' and I wanted to live purposefully. Thinking professionally helped me achieve that.

When you think about it, being a mother of young children is rather like doing at least three or four professional jobs all at the same time. You are a nurse, a taxi-driver, an entertainer, a cleaner, a cook, a nutritionist and a psychologist with perhaps a few other roles thrown in. Because these multi-functional roles have never been adequately recognised, manufacturers have never seriously turned their attention to producing truly labour-saving devices for mothers of small children. Why isn't our 'profession' supported by the production of such useful items as a non-spill mug for Mum's tea that doesn't look as though it was made for an invalid? Or how about a pre-stained sweatshirt? That way we could wear a dribble of posset over our left shoulder and know about it. Why has no-one ever manufactured coffee-flavoured toothpaste? With time in the bathroom being at such a premium we could get one chore accomplished and get that vital early dose of caffeine! Finally, and this is my 'pièce de résistance' (develop this and I'll claim copyright), why don't they magnetise every tiny piece of Lego/Duplo/Sticklebricks, etc. and provide you with some sort of magnetic shovel to pick it all up with?

It seems to me that the heads of industry have very little idea about how life runs for someone looking after small children. The people who do know and understand are those who have been there. They have the best suggestions and the most helpful advice to offer. It is to these people I have turned for the advice in the second half of this chapter, by drawing on the experience and collating the suggestions from all the woman who completed the questionnaire.

We've seen how early motherhood can make us feel. Let's now turn our attention to how we can make a success of this season of our lives. For the sake of simplicity I've divided our vocation into four broad professional roles.

The Nutritionist

Nutrition. Now here's a subject fraught with guilt and anxiety. First of all, there's the issue of 'Will they eat or won't they?' Children generally fall into three categories: the non-eaters ('He won't eat a thing') the faddy eaters (they like chicken nuggets one day and can't bear them the next) and the piggy eaters (self-explanatory). All of them drive their mothers up the wall with anxiety although for different reasons.

I can testify to the existence of 'non-eaters' because I was related to one. My nephew ate no more than a yoghurt and a biscuit for most meals for a period of time exceeding a year. Food did not interest him in the least and all efforts to entice him were in vain or counter-productive. Eventually and very slowly he did broaden his repertoire of acceptable foods and is now a bright, intelligent young man, seemingly suffering no ill effects from his earlier eating habits.

For parents of children in the second two categories the issue is not whether they will eat but 'What *do* they eat?' and 'What *should* they eat?' The answers to these two questions are frequently opposed to one another. For some children, food is a life and death issue: the life and death of the chicken/fish/pig on the plate being the one in question. For quite a long time my children believed that the Sunday chicken was something that came out of the chicken (like the egg) without the chicken noticing anything. I can't honestly say I rushed to contradict this helpful, if rather over-optimistic view of a chicken carcass.

If your children are sensitive in this direction you cannot have a meal that looks or sounds like animal parts (although curiously enough if it's shaped like dinosaurs it's perfectly edible). So lamb chops and tongue are definitely off the menu. Fish fingers are okay because everyone knows fish don't have fingers, but woe betide you if you serve up a real fish, complete with staring eye!

Even vegetables aren't safe from this kind of dilemma. I once grew some cress with my son's assistance. We did it as a sort of lesson in nurture and nutrition all rolled into one. After a week's careful watering and watching, the morning came when he opted for cheese and cress sandwiches (the more traditional egg and cress combination being impossible given his aversion to eggs). This was a brave request for a small boy for whom all vegetable matter is a total anathema. I showed him how to harvest his cress but no sooner had the first bunch been snipped and slipped into his cheese sandwich than it suddenly occurred to him.

'Does cress die, Mummy?'

I was faced with a choice. If I said 'yes' the chances of him actually now consuming a *dead* cress and cheese sandwich seemed rather remote. Then again, if I said 'no' what could be more alarming than 'live' vegetable matter wriggling in your tummy? I told the truth and sure enough the sandwich was spurned. I couldn't really argue with him, after all he had spent a week lovingly nurturing the cress he'd just slain.

I guess we all have friends whose children will eat raw vegetables. The children of a friend of mine will only eat them raw. They probably do this because their parents eat vegetables this way. This puts me under terrible condemnation because try as I might I feel very unpassionate about raw carrots.

Anyway, let's not linger over this guilt-ridden subject. Here's the advice about small children and food, my remarks in italics:

- Don't make a fuss over food. Once children see that they can get you worked up and anxious they will use this to their advantage. Food should never be an 'issue', it should be a pleasure.
- Don't compare what one child will eat with what a more adventurous child will try.
- Even if the child doesn't like food much, make meal times relaxing, enjoyable events with a nicely laid table and time to talk or play afterwards.
- Don't make rules you can't keep. *The rule, 'No dessert if you don't finish your dinner' lead to a lot of gagging and resentment in our house. We adapted it to 'You get the same proportion of dessert as you managed to eat of your*

first course' i.e., if you eat a lot of dinner, you get a lot of pud (our children will probably turn out fat but happy!).
- Remember life is more than food.

Household Manager

There are a lot of less attractive titles for the tasks summed up by this phrase but you can supply these for yourselves. This subject will be covered in more detail in a later chapter but as small children are notorious for disrupting the smooth running of the household I thought it would be worth mentioning a few suggestions at this point gleaned from those in the know, again my remarks in italics:

- Divide your day up into manageable bits, e.g., morning/afternoon/evening and only attempt one task/activity or outing in each section. *Is she kidding? One task per day was often my limit.*
- Get the children to help with the chores, give them dusters and small Hoovers. You have to accept the fact that their interest in this game will not coincide with yours nor will they 'play' cleaning for half the length of time you need to clean. If they do 'help', accept that the job will take twice the time.
- Alternate between a chore and a game, 'We'll do a puzzle and then I'll make your bed.' *You have to keep your promises on this one. If the child follows you around all day in expectation of the promised activity and is disappointed, you've blown it for the next time.*
- Ten minutes of focused attention on the children setting up an activity or generating a game may well result in twenty minutes peace, so don't be tempted to say, 'Go and play.' It'll pay you to help them get started.
- Cook in bulk if you can. It doesn't take much longer and you can put half away for another time.
- Have a place or time that is your place to relax. One of

the problems for a mother of young children is that your home becomes your workplace so you never get that pleasant feeling of coming home and 'clocking off'.

- Don't set your standards too high. There will be much more time later on in life to have a tidy house. *'Untidiness is not life-threatening', wrote one of my correspondents. True, but if it really bothers you, it may threaten your sanity. If you can't stop it bothering you, find some easy routine for dealing with chores early in the day so you are free to get on with more important things.*

- Reduce work to a minimum. *If you're the type that needs to wash the net curtains every six weeks then don't have net curtains. One friend admitted to me with the air of a conspirator, 'I don't iron socks and pants any more.' 'Oh, really?' I said, trying to hide my amusement. It has never in my life occurred to me to iron socks and pants. For a while in our house all that got ironed was shirt collars.*

Social Organiser

This broad description covers the whole range of things you do to enable your child to acclimatise socially.

Coffee Mornings

Some people have the idea that mothers at home with small children spend ridiculous amounts of time having friends round for coffee and idle conversation. The truth is there is no such thing as an idle conversation with small children around. Coffee is drunk standing up because we know if we sit down we'll have to stand up again as soon as Jenny needs a wee/trips over the toy car/head-butts the floor. This last feat was achieved by my son attempting to reach his ankles with his hands down the inside of a baggy pair of trousers. Considering the resulting loss of balance, it was unfortunate that he wasn't standing on a carpet at the time.

No, coffee mornings are not idle opportunities for relaxation and stimulating conversation. The art of conversation around small children is the art of remembering what it was you were saying five minutes previously and carrying on as if you hadn't just had to remove all the books on the lower shelves to 'higher ground'. In this situation you don't need to know how to finish a conversation because a small child can be guaranteed to do that for you. Writing as someone who has recently emerged from this season, I have found I have had to re-learn the art of ending conversations as up until now awkward pauses or uncertain moments have been inevitably filled by someone wanting their shoes put on or their bottom wiped!

Toddler Groups

These can either be friendly places of refuge where you can meet people who understand, and someone else can make the coffee; or they can be a nightmare because no-one talks to you, or because your child turns out to be a thumper or a biter. (If the latter is true the former almost certainly will be, but it ought not be that way). As a Toddler Group leader, naturally I believe in the value of such groups. The ideal place is friendly; big enough for small kids to run around in; and has a good variety of quality toys. The best way to use such groups is to go regularly because then you get to know people. Also, rather than just dropping into a chair for a chat, aim to do something with your child. This is worth the effort and it especially pays off with clingy children. These groups are an important stepping stone.

Nursery

By the time your eldest is in a nursery or playgroup you may well have another one on the way or in the push-chair. Delicate negotiations ae called for so that the older child

doesn't feel that he is being marched out of the door and
abandoned somewhere simply because a younger child has
arrived. If you get over that hurdle, nursery's great,
especially if you don't have to pay for it, and still worth
considering if you do. If the cost of playgroup or nursery
puts them out of the question then a cheaper and convenient
alternative is 'child-swapping'. Find a friend with compatible
children and you have hers for two hours a week in your
home with your children and then she has yours back later
in the week so that you both get two hours off. This
arrangement needs to be reciprocal and ought to be started
on a trial basis so that you can back off with dignity if need
be. All of these are further steps up the social ladder to the
biggest of all hurdles.

School

Of course, you don't have to send your child to school but,
if you decide that home education is not for you, I do have
to warn you that the hardest part of sending them to school
is getting them there with all the relevant bits of paper,
reading books, lunch-boxes, PE kits, etc. All this has to be
organised before 9 a.m. It can often leave me feeling finished
off before the day's hardly begun.

At one stage I had to provide a small amount of money in
a named purse each morning so that my daughter could
purchase a drink. The effort of having to remember those
pennies, combined with the effort of actually trying to find
them, all added up to a lot of hassle. Why was it that
whenever I was raking around for another 2p, all I could
find was the plastic play money from the toy cash till? These
nasty little pieces of plastic get everywhere. I've often been
sorely tempted to enclose the odd 'toy town tuppence' to
make up the required amount. (It adds a whole new meaning
to the phrase, 'Do you take plastic?')

Before we move on from the role of social organiser,
there are also many other environments to which a socially

adept child must learn to adapt, each with its own set of preferred behaviour. These vary from the church crèche (no wailing), to visits to Gran's (no rude words), to water-confidence classes (no bowel movements, please!). How far you get on the social scene with your small children in tow depends largely on your own courage and willpower.

Finally, we come to the profession that occupies a major part of any mother's time. It is a little hard to define so you'll have to excuse the rather wordy title:

Psychologist/Disciplinarian/Politician/ Spiritual Advisor

This is meant to sum up our duty to understand, nurture, guide and discipline our offspring towards some accepted standard of behaviour and consideration toward, not merely the wider world (difficult enough), but also toward their younger sister (almost impossible?).

I think that it is for this part of the job that most of us who are not trained in any of these professions feel an acute lack of qualifications. (Although I suspect even for those so trained, reality may conflict with their theories.) Well, help is at hand. I have the combined wisdom of a group of women for whom disobedience is not a problem! Out of the five suggested problems that we encounter in our role as mother, those who completed the questionnaires rated 'disobedience' as the least problematic. Their biggest problem was 'lack of time' closely followed by 'untidiness', 'sibling squabbling', 'their own emotional or physical state', and finally 'disobedience'. I take that to mean that some of these suggestions must work.

However, before I launch into a list of prescriptive suggestions, I'd like to make a plea for flexibility. Every child and every family is different, so what works for one person may not work for another. There is no easy recipe for producing pleasant, polite, diligent children. We're all just doing our best and we need to have the humility to listen to others with respect and be prepared to change course if necessary.

We did an about-turn on a discipline issue recently. After several years of trying every method I'd heard of to deal with childish tantrums, I found it wonderfully liberating to realise that one perfectly valid 'method' was not to deal with them at all but, instead, to completely ignore the child in question and the bad behaviour. We'd tried smacking, sending them to their room, sending them to the stairs, all to no avail; and then it dawned on us that all these methods involved us in an interaction with the child. They also ensured that the tantrumming child commanded our full attention. Nobody had ever told me that I had a 'right to remain silent'. Everything I read or heard about pushed me to 'deal with it' to 'do something' or to 'confront and win' or else risk failure. I found that it was, in fact, far more effective to simply remove my positive attention. I say 'simply', but ignoring a tantrumming child can be very hard. It means instantly averting your gaze and carrying on as if the child were not there. It takes a lot of concentration. If the tantrum gets so bad that the child is endangering himself, his sibling or the fabric of his home then obviously you have to intervene, but you can still do so in as calm and non-reactive a way as possible, not making eye contact while restraining the child or putting him in a safer place.

Positive attention has to be worth something in the first place if the removal of it is going to have any affect. Heaps of positive attention during the normal run of the day can often be the best preventative measure against tantrums. But nothing is guaranteed to work. Tantrums in small children are often irrational. One of my children used to get angry when her cracker biscuit broke on the first bite. As it was now a 'broken biscuit', it was deemed uncomsumable. In the face of such logic, patience will serve you better than reason.

So here, with apologies for the preamble, is the collected

wisdom of a group of women who didn't have a problem with discipline. There is no meaning intended in the order in which these come. My remarks in italics as before.

- The way you say what you have to say is as important as what you say. *Read that aloud a few times and it will eventually make sense.*
- Pray, pray, pray.
- Look at your kids when you talk to them. They'll hear you better.
- Set aside time to spend with each child individually
- Lower your expectations about their standard of behaviour. Be prepared to allow a certain degree of bad behaviour. Don't overreact.
- Stick to your rules on obedience and don't give in. *This appears to contradict the previous remark. See what I mean about flexibility.*
- Have friends that you can talk and pray with.
- Sleep in the afternoon if you need to.
- Admit your need and accept help.
- Sibling squabbling often arises from boredom. *In other words, identify the cause not just the problem.*
- Sibling squabbling probably doesn't bother them as much as it bothers you.
- Distract or ignore if you can. Save confrontations for issues that really matter.
- Separate sulky, bad-tempered children.
- Take physical factors into account when you are dealing with a fractious child. Is she hungry? Ill? Tired?
- Refuse to hear tale-telling unless the two squabblers have agreed the story between themselves. *If they ever agree about what happened they'll probably have sorted it out for themselves. On similar lines to this I refuse to allow a video to go on until they have peacefully negotiated which one it's to be.*
- If you postpone a decision don't be drawn into an early commitment. *'We'll see' is my failing in this area. My*

children take it to mean, 'I'll say yes in a minute if you don't keep on at me'.

- Light a candle in the kitchen or at a meal-time as a reminder of the presence of Christ.

The final suggestion for this chapter is not solely related to the role of disciplinarian but is good advice generally for anyone in the season of early motherhood: don't ignore your own needs. You may not always be able to have them met but you must not think that they are wrong. Our children invade our lives at this stage and things like personal space, sleep and intellectual stimulation are at a premium. You may have to forego these things for a while but you are not a bad mother just because you are looking forward to the day when you can claim some of these things back.

Chapter 3

Motherhood: The Redcoat Stage

Today's package holiday 'rep' is probably the modern equivalent of the old-fashioned holiday camp entertainer known as a Redcoat. The job of the Redcoat or 'rep' is to exude endless enthusiasm, organise non-stop entertainment and resolve difficult dilemmas with diplomatic ease – all this in a hot climate while wearing a perfectly pressed outfit with a radiant smile permanently pasted in place.

Who'd be a holiday 'rep?' Only cheerful, resilient, well-organised types need apply. When you consider the similarities between the job description for a 'Redcoat' and that of the average mother with school-age children, it is not hard to see why so many of us find this stage of motherhood such hard going.

There is a myth amongst mothers of preschool children that 'life gets easier once they go to school'. I remember believing this myth. I felt envious of all that 'free' time enjoyed by mums with older children. I couldn't believe my ears when they talked about the tyranny of that three o'clock deadline at the school gates. How could anyone be rushed to collect the children on time when they'd just enjoyed six hours of uninterrupted peace?

Now my children are both at school, I realise that while perhaps in one sense life gets easier there is a very real sense in which it gets more complicated. We face bigger decisions about how to use those six hours each day and our expectations about what can be achieved rocket to previously unimagined heights. We try to tackle everything and we still find that there aren't enough hours in the day for all the unpaid 'voluntary' activities such as cooking, cleaning, gar-

dening, ironing, writing letters; let alone time enough for
the possibility of paid labour during those few school hours.

That inflexible mid-afternoon deadline puts paid to any
impulse days out. It cuts short any long lunches with friends.
The school timetable leaves us with a short day chopped in
two parts by lunch. We get a decent period of time in the
morning, an indifferent period of time in the afternoon and
then an even shorter time with the children before teatime
and bedtime (yours or theirs depending on the age of your
children). Into these few hours at the end of the day we are
still trying to cram all the physical and emotional nourish-
ment that we want to give our children while at the same
time taking them to one or two after-school clubs and
activities to 'broaden their horizons'.

It probably is rather churlish of me to complain about the
brevity of six child-free hours a day. After all, I wouldn't
want the school day to be any longer. In a sense it's not the
amount of time that is the problem. It's the fact that the time
comes to us broken up into shorter chunks. When you know
you've only got two hours to get stuck into a task it can be
very disheartening. You forget what can be achieved and
focus on the fact that by 3 p.m. the desk/sewing-machine/
wallpaper and paint will all have to be cleared away.

There is also the fact that all this time arrives like a
sudden windfall. Just as one has to make more responsible
decisions with larger sums of money, so you have to make
more responsible decisions when you find yourself with
larger amounts of time. Bear in mind that when you first
become a Redcoat mum you are just emerging from that
free and easy stage of life where decisions were largely
dictated to you by your child's needs and you will realise
that responsible decision making is no longer your forte.

If you are now the mother of school-age children you may
not have compared yourself to a Redcoat but it is probably
true that you are responsible for all the arrangements for
your child's educational life, and for a large part of their
social life (as a taxi-driver, if nothing else). You are simul-

taneously responsible for their nurture: spiritually and emotionally. In an ideal situation these responsibilities are shared jointly with your spouse but they are still huge responsibilities and added to them are the minor ones such as being 'the only member of the household who knows where everything is', 'the person who remembers Gran's birthday' and 'the only one who talks to the canary or walks the dog'. The sense of being 'all things to all people' is absolutely overwhelming at this stage of life. Just as you think you are beginning to handle the situation, the children's bedtimes get later and you wave good-bye to another chunk of personal space. The scenery is constantly shifting. All this at a time when your own personal horizons are expected to broaden and expand because, according to the world out there, 'you've got so much time on your hands'.

Other people's expectations of you reach a peak during your youngest child's first year at school. You are finally 'free' to come in and hear children read. You can go on the church cleaning rota, you could help out in voluntary groups. The list of possibilities is endless. If you have been successfully juggling some paid employment before the children went to school, the expectation for you to increase your hours is almost irresistible. There is nothing wrong with any of these options. The problem is that there are so many of them. At this time, more than at any other, there is a need to be pro-active, doing what you believe is right for you to be doing, not reactive which simply means opting into any and every passing opportunity.

Once you have settled on what your main 'calling' is – a vocation outside the home, a voluntary task that you can balance with time at home, further training or whatever – the picture becomes a bit clearer. Having decided what you are going to do it is easier to see what you are not going to be able to do and make appropriate arrangements. For example, if paid employment leaves no time to clean, employ a cleaner. Some responsibilities can be given away in this fashion but the Redcoat vocation will not go away so let's now turn our attention to the demands and dilemmas that this stage of our lives presents to us.

Asked what aspect of motherhood drained them the most, my Redcoat correspondents cited the following: selfish teenage behaviour; constant criticism from offspring; sibling rivalry; the assumption that Mum knows everything and does everything; constant noise in the house; no time for personal life/hobbies; no personal space with spouse. This list makes rather grim reading but my correspondents were as equally generous with their solutions and suggestions as they were in their complaints.

The big issues for mothers at this stage generally divide into one of two categories: practical matters or policy matters. The first relates to what children do, wear and who they hang about with. The second relates to matters that have some kind of moral dimension: sex education, money matters, and the encouraging of socially acceptable behaviour. It helps to have a policy about these kinds of issue and I have several on offer, all gleaned from women who are learning to spin this plate effectively.

Practical Issues

Clubbing

No, not dancing till 2 a.m. I mean after-school clubs or week-end activities such as swimming lessons, gymnastics, riding lessons, drama classes, piano lessons and so on. As these are all fairly expensive and 'interest-based', you are well advised to only go for those activities that truly interest your child. If you are going to be warmly supportive and enthusiastic it would help to be fairly interested in the skill/sport yourself. Don't take your child to any activity just because you feel you ought to and certainly not because it's fashionable or because someone else's child goes. Mind you, if 'someone else's child' does go, make the most of the opportunity to share lifts. Apart from the expense and hassle factor of getting them there and back each of these activities claims another chunk of their time and yours as well as a big proportion of their energy.

For all of these reasons I'd say that six-'ish', depending on your child, is early enough to start anything, and that for a younger child one weekly activity may be enough in addition to the full school day. Be led by your child's interest and enthusiasm. Don't send him to judo 'to toughen him up' if his real interest is the natural world, and don't send her riding just because you loved it when you were a child. It's only worth paying for an out-of-school class if your child is genuinely enthusiastic and only then for as long as the enthusiasm lasts. Once they lose interest, drop the activity without any acrimony over 'the waste of money' and reflect on how their experience of life has been broadened.

So far my daughter has done two terms of swimming, one term of dancing and three terms of recorders. The swimming badges were earned so fast at the outset that I began to harbour notions of 'child prodigy' and gold medals; but now it seems I'll have to settle for a good all-rounder. Beware of being a pushy parent. The purpose of these clubs is to broaden the child's experience and strengthen their confidence, not necessarily to set them on the path to greatness.

A word about badges. These are the hidden cost behind the termly outlay. Children love them. They give a great sense of progress, but you've got to fork out for them and you've got to sew them on to something. Handy hint: sew swimming badges on to a large new towel, big enough to last the duration of their swimming career. In the case of gymnastics, put the badges on a tee-shirt several sizes too large for the child in the hope that by the time they've outgrown the shirt they'll have outgrown the activity.

Brownies/Beavers/Scouts/Girls' Brigade

These are all essentially character-forming 'social' clubs. Their value doesn't just lie in what they will teach your children and their quality is often strongly linked to the quality of the leadership so only you can take a decision as to the value of your local groups.

Dress Sense

At a certain age, clothes become a policy issue. Under that age they are a practical issue. Children need to be kept warm, comfortable and decent. Some children are opinionated about clothes from the moment they learn to take off unacceptable items. Other children remain indifferent to the issue until well into their teens. Allowing them to choose what to wear each day can be a helpful first responsibility. It can also be the only way to preserve one's sanity with a child who rejects your every choice outright. If you have a child who is totally clueless about clothes giving them a limited choice will at least avoid the 'sleeveless top in midwinter' scenario. If you give free choice then you must be prepared to close your eyes to the wonderful clashes and combinations that are preferred. In general, an attitude of benign indifference with a ounce of suggestion is all that is necessary. If you encourage fashion consciousness in your 'frilly filly' too early you make a rod for your own back. It will come soon enough. Meanwhile your unselfconscious, unco-ordinated 'rag-bag' will be easier to live with than a fussy follower of fashion.

Once clothes do become a policy issue, opt for the simplest policy. 'You want it? You pay for it' is one possibility, as is a clear definition of the minimum standard of decency. Beyond these two bench-marks all you have to try to remember is that it is the person inside the clothes, or under the hairstyle, who needs your affirmation and love. Don't get too distracted by outward appearances.

Pets

All children hanker after a pet at some time or another. If you don't already have one don't give in to the first 'hankering'! Pets can enrich family life in many ways but they also have big drawbacks. Who will walk it? Feed it? Clean out its cage? All these issues ought to be settled first but the combined experience of many mothers suggests that no matter how faithfully the children promise to do these things you should not believe them. If you buy a pet without accepting the fact that ultimately the buck stops with you, then you will be quickly disillusioned. Dogs and cats are only for those seriously committed to long-term pet owner-ship. Dogs require long walks and both dogs and cats hike up your grocery bill. On the plus side, they will become part of your family in a way that a hamster never will and a dog who adores you is a huge ego boost. It may only be cupboard love but on days when unquestioning loyalty and uncondi-tional love are felt to be in short supply, even that provided by a dog can come in handy for parent or child.

Hamsters are nocturnal. This makes them a little disap-pointing in terms of daytime companionship. Rabbits will dig holes in your lawn, guinea-pigs don't. Guinea-pigs are cylindrical eating machines on very short legs. They make amusing noises, they don't jump or dig, they can live outside, they're not smelly – in fact they have quite a lot going for them in the 'ideal pet' stakes.

Peers

These are not as easily controlled as pets and may even come into the other 'P' category: pests! Peers are those children who are roughly the same age as your children, with whom they rub shoulders at school, in the street or in church. They are not all pests by any means but nor are they always friends. Whatever they are they have to be reckoned with as a significant source of influence on your child: 'Sally's allowed to . . .', 'Mark says it's okay to . . .' etc. There isn't an awful lot you can do regarding your children's choice of friends other than stand by supportively and be on hand for the 'fall-out'. You can provide a wide circle of potential friends for your child to relate to but you cannot force your child to befriend your best friend's child even though this would be convenient. They have to make their own choices and learn the hard way about how relationships are made, sustained and sometimes broken.

They can choose their friends but they have no choice over their relatives. This fact will become clear when they no longer wish to be seen walking round town with you. It may hurt to suddenly find yourself to be a public embarrassment as far as your offspring is concerned but you can console yourself that privately you will always be 'Mum'. I once heard someone remark, wisely, that it is a mistake for a mother to try to become her daughter's 'best friend'. A girl can have any number of best friends with whom to follow fashion and discuss 'local talent' but she has only one Mum. So when your offspring no longer deem you to be in vogue, don't wobble in your sense of security. Yours is a fixed and unchanging role. You are 'Mum', and that's what you'll always be. That isn't an excuse not to inform yourself about youth culture and language. You need to stay in touch, but you don't have to be 'hip'.

Policy Issues

For some issues it is extremely helpful to have a policy decided in advance. Once decided, a policy helps to avoid interminable wrangling and heated negotiations (although both of these will be part of the policy making process) but it must never be set in stone. It will need rewording and reworking regularly to reapply it to the changing situations as the children grow. Trade unions have policies on ageism, racism, sexism, and overtime. Families need policies on rather smaller issues such as pocket money, chores and television rights.

Money

From very early on children become aware that money plays a very important part in our lives. They overhear remarks such as, 'We can't afford it', or 'They must be made of money' or 'Wait till the end of the month' and draw their own conclusions as to the power of this commodity. At first they have no comprehension of the amount of money required to do certain things. No sooner had my children heard about Disneyland than they immediately and nobly offered to forego their weekly pocket money 'if Mummy and Daddy could take them there, please'. The money issue is often complicated by our own hang-ups about what we need/desire or about what we'd like to provide for our children but can't afford.

Whatever your policy on money, I suggest it should encompass two principles: first, that money is merely a neutral tool, not good, not bad, but simply a means to an end. Second, that if money is handled responsibly it ought to go further (sadly not always true, in today's society shrewd managers still struggle).

In order to get across the first point you have to give them enough pocket money/allowance for them to really learn to exercise responsibility. A six-year-old with 8p a week won't even be able to afford a third of a chocolate bar come Saturday. It might seem pious and unworldly to give stingy amounts of pocket money but there are good reasons for being as generous as you can. If they get 'toy town' amounts they will think money is just play stuff but if you are as generous as is reasonable you are entrusting them with the responsibility of choice.

Teaching them the second principle is harder. You have to stand back and grit your teeth while they spend their hoarded amount on the object of their desires. If it is a particularly nasty piece of plastic trivia which will break after five minutes, you will have to bite your tongue. If they have set their heart on it and staked their 50p for it, they

will have to learn the hard way. Earning is a useful way to
enhance this process of devolved responsibility. An extra
chore 'beyond the call of normal duty' can be linked to
financial incentives.

Before we leave the subject of money it is worth pointing
out that as the 'pocket pennies for Saturday treats' turn into
a monthly allowance there should be a corresponding
increase in the number of things that the offspring are meant
to buy for themselves. Depending on your child's age and
the amount of money involved, the sort of things they might
reasonably be expected to pay for themselves range from
clothes to toiletries, computer games and CDs, from stamps
to phone calls. When the telephone companies finally
brought in itemised bills this was a huge boon to some good
friends of ours. At the time they had two teenage daughters,
one of whom was given to making long distance calls at 4
p.m. The itemised bill allowed the parents to process an
individual bill for each daughter. The first bill for the
younger one came to an amount well over her monthly
allowance. It took her three months to pay off this debt but
it was amazing how quickly she learnt the meaning of the
words 'cheap rate'.

Television Rights

This is not the right of any family member to televise the
internal workings of the family but rather the rights of
family members to watch a certain amount of television
each week. It is another example of an issue that is often
fraught and guilt-ridden. 'Are they watching "too much"?'
'How much is "too much"?' and 'What are they watching?'
seem to be the major concerns. Whatever policy you aim
for, two principles seem vital: improve their critical faculties
and teach them how to use the 'off' knob.

A few people simply opt out of this debate altogether and
have no TV in the home. At first glance, this seems noble
and courageous but it isn't always. Only if your family is

honestly disinterested in what's on the box should you find other ways to spend your TV licence money. If they are interested then the 'no TV' option is a 'head in the sand' approach to the issue. Children can never learn to control an influence if they are never exposed to that influence. Instead of raising our hands in horror I think we need to accept that our children are growing up in a TV and computer age, and that the more constructive approach is to equip them to handle these influences.

Besides, television can cultivate critical faculties. When I was a teenager I took a friend to see her first feature film. It was a soppy musical. This friend had grown up without a television and she sobbed her way through the entire film. She had never developed the critical distance that would have enabled her to say, 'It's only a story'. It might be argued that the same critical distance means that violence or true-life tragedy are also dulled in their impact and children become immune to things that ought to shock. Because this is possible the only thing to do is discuss what is on and why they want to watch it, not in a confrontational way but in a constructive way that helps them to make their own decisions. If you cannot dissuade them from watching a trashy cartoon at least sit down with them and watch it together. Other helpful rules of thumb are: turn the TV off at the end of each programme and don't turn it on until you've looked in the paper to see what is on that's worth watching.

Another form of control is to establish certain times of the day when the TV goes on. Perhaps while supper's being cooked (for your benefit) or after lunch (for their benefit). This last idea works best when you can use a video recorder to record worthwhile programmes to show at the times when it is convenient to watch something.

The television is not the great enemy. It can be a helpful source of information, ideas and entertainment, but it does need to be controlled. It is only fair to acknowledge that we all enjoy TV as a way to relax. One friend of mine makes allowance for this by permitting a 'couch potato' programme every now and again. Other suggested means of control are not allowing a television in bedrooms (including your own) in order to discourage the isolation of an addict, and not allowing any television during meal-times. This sends the message that spending time talking with each other is far more important. One of my correspondents with four sons and one television passed on the following trio of tips:

- Give each child a certain number of television tokens. One token equals one hour or one type of programme, e.g., nature/children's/film/documentary. They can spend these tokens as they like but have to negotiate with the others who is going to watch what and pay their tokens into named boxes on top of the set as they are used up. At the end of the week the boxes are opened and tokens retrieved for the next week.
- Have a book for people to write down what they've recorded on which tape with a column for them to tick when they've viewed it. (*Well-organised or what?*)
- Glue all the remote control devices on to a large piece of wood. That way they won't get lost down the back of the sofa.

This woman's policy obviously worked for her and involved the children admirably in problem-solving techniques, negotiation, record-keeping, and even weight-lifting! Your policy may be much simpler but if it works for you, that's fine.

Discipline

This part of our Redcoat role can be a trial in every sense of the word. Sometimes we are the judge, handing out sentences ('No television for two days'), sometimes we are the judge, handing out sentences ('No television for two days'), sometimes we are the jury assessing the blame ('I know he was annoying you but should you really have thumped him?'). At other times you are the prosecutor trying to bring a conviction of wrong-doing to an unrepentant villain, and sometimes you are the counsel for the defence ('She didn't really mean it. If you hadn't beheaded her Barbie doll, she'd have probably left you in peace.'). A successful policy for this area of life does two things: it tells you how to prevent unnecessary confrontations and second it tells you what to do when confrontations occur, as they inevitably will.

One helpful tool in the promotion of good behaviour and the prevention of bad is the chart – not a 'pop chart' or a 'sailing chart' but a plain old-fashioned star chart. To some families this idea will be a total anathema. You might never have tried a chart, feeling that the whole idea of reaping a reward for good behaviour is rather at odds with the unconditional love you are called to give your child. Well, in part, you're right. We don't just love our kids because they behave well or succeed, but giving credit for good behaviour doesn't have to communicate a conditional response to the child.

There are two apparently opposing ideas that we need to communicate to our children. One is, 'You shall reap what you sow' – in other words, 'Your behaviour does matter, it does have consequences.' The second is, 'I'll love you forever' – in other words, 'No matter what you do I'll always love you.'

If you use a chart carefully it can demonstrate very effectively the first of these ideas. It works especially well with younger children who want to see a tangible result for their good behaviour. You can, for example, list which chores are to be done by whom and leave a space for a large satisfying tick when the chore is completed.

Charts work on the principle, 'Don't expect, inspect'. Far from being a means of patronising a child, they can be a means of giving credit where it's due, a way of expressing appreciation, of drawing attention to the child's efforts. All of these 'positive strokes' are a powerful incentive for each child to pull their weight as part of the family team.

Some people have objected to charts on the basis that
they manipulate behaviour. Well, yes they do. But if you
substitute the words 'direct', 'train' or 'modify' for that
loaded word 'manipulate' you will find that that is what we
are called to do as parents. Manipulating seems to imply
that we try to change our behaviour for our own ends but in
fact directing their behaviour is a legitimate part of our
calling to 'train up a child in the way they should go'.

'Good behaviour' is a curiously indefinable thing. I
realised some time ago that too often I left my children to
work out for themselves what 'good behaviour' looked like.
If they had to judge it by working out the things I reacted to
they might conclude that 'good behaviour' meant being
compliant or simply being quiet. I realised it wasn't very
satisfactory simply telling them to 'be good' without defining
for them what that type of behaviour entailed. I devised a
three-fold definition of good behaviour which I put into a
chart. Each part started with the verb, 'Be'. I did this
because I didn't want a pharisaical list of right and wrong
actions. Behaving well is much more about who you are
rather than what you do. So I settled on three simple things
to aim for: Be Cheerful, Be Kind, Be Helpful. It isn't hard
to find a scripture verse to back up each of these injunctions
if you are that way inclined. I wrote these three on a chart
and illustrated them with a line drawing so that they'd make
sense for my non-reader. I also padded them out with a few
specifics such as 'Be Kind' means 'no' to squabbling and
fighting and 'yes' to hugs and encouragement. Under 'Be
Helpful' we devised an appropriate task for each of them.
'Be Cheerful' meant a limit on whining and trying to be a
good loser. All this was drawn on plain paper, stuck on a
piece of cardboard and then covered with sticky-back plastic. The clear plastic means you can tick and erase whenever
you want, using a felt-tip pen.

This system was simply a reward and appreciation chart.
The only negative possibility was not to receive a tick in a
certain column. Charts are meant to monitor positive pro-

gress so they need to be simple enough to guarantee the child will succeed, otherwise he just gets disheartened.

'Negative reinforcement' is that part of your policy that tells you what to do when conflict has arisen. It is whatever you choose to do when your child misbehaves in a way that warrants a negative reaction from you, such as a sanction or a time-out period. Sanctions that are immediate, effective and not degrading are the most useful. We dock portions of pocket money, although we do allow a chance to earn it back. We use time-outs in the bedroom and no doubt we shall come on to the technique known as 'grounding'. To sum up all the advice about negative ways to curb bad behaviour, the most popular method seemed to be the sanction: the reasonable withholding of something desirable (sweets, TV, money, personal liberty) for a predetermined time having warned in advance that this would happen if misbehaviour was repeated.

One final version of a chart that often proves very useful is the one by the front door listing all the different things each child has to take to school on each day (dinner money, gym kit, reading books). This is an invaluable aid for any mother who, like me finds it hard at such an early hour to know what day of the week it is, let alone what item of kit they are meant to be carrying into school. Better still get the children to make the chart *and* check it.

As if all these practical issues and policy issues weren't enough for the average Redcoat mother, we haven't yet discussed the largest responsibility of all, that of education. For most of us our responsibility to educate is largely fulfilled when we've found the right school, purchased the right uniform and got them to the right place at the right time. This isn't as easy as it sounds and choosing a school for your child can be an agonising decision of awesome dimensions.

There are three areas to consider when you are looking at schools: the education on offer, the ethos, and convenience of location. The educational questions are things like, 'Is the school strong on sports or music?' or 'Will my child be able to learn two languages if she is so inclined?' Only you can know what you are looking for when you have assessed the needs and abilities of your child. But even if you do make such an assessment you may not have a suitable place available locally or the factors of ethos and convenience may be more important. Ethos is the general atmosphere of the school, the attitude of the staff. Is it a friendly 'we're-all-in-this-together' type of place or is it a keen 'every-child-for-itself' type of place? Which do you want? Finally don't overlook convenience of location as an important factor. If your child has to take two tedious bus journeys each way to school and back or if you have to run a second car purely for the school run, it needs to be worth it. The distance will probably mean the child will have few friends locally and home-school links will be harder to maintain.

'Education' and 'school' are two words that tend to go hand in hand but that doesn't have to be the case. Some parents these days are opting out of school altogether and choosing 'home education'. For me, the primary two benefits of this would be not having to get out by 9 a.m. and not having to make sandwich lunches. After that I'd be listing drawbacks such as the difficulty of being 'Mum' and 'teacher' simultaneously and the problem of withdrawing the children from what is essentially a common cultural experience. I take my hat off to those people who do it successfully but it isn't possible or even appropriate for all of us. So if it isn't for you, don't worry. There are still two other parts of your child's education which remain with you. These are sex education and spiritual education.

Schools do, of course, offer both and I whole-heartedly encourage you to inform yourself about your school's policy. Since 1993 all maintained schools must publish a policy on sex education. You can even involve yourself with the forming of this policy by becoming a parent governor. All secondary schools must teach it and the law states that sex education must 'encourage young people to have regard to moral considerations and the value of family life'. You are allowed to withdraw your child if you prefer. In practise it is likely that the curriculum on offer will cover the mechanics of sex and contraception very thoroughly and leave the moral dimension largely unexplored. The former won't do your child any harm but you may want to compensate for the latter.

Why wait until they are eleven anyway? By the age of seven, let alone eleven, most children will have discovered 'the facts of life' from someone in the playground. If they hear it from someone else you cannot control whatever attitude is passed on with the information (for example, sex is dirty secret) nor can you be on hand to allay fears or answer questions. It's not a bad idea to get in first with the information in a low-key way with a good book that's appropriate to their age (such as Malcolm and Meryl Doney, *Who Made Me?* illustrated by N. Butterworth and M. Inkpen, Marshall Pickering, 1987). Some people say wait until they ask but you don't wait until your child asks about road safety before you teach him to cross the road. Admittedly they cross roads far younger than they have sexual relationships but when you think about it, a child's whole life is lived out within the framework of sexual relationships: the parent's relationship, the grandparent's ('which Granny had Mummy?'). So why be secretive? If you think you are depriving them of their innocence by telling them how they were conceived the implication is that you think sex is not a good gift from God but some sort of unsavoury necessity of reproduction.

Besides, it is not just explaining 'the plumbing' that matters at this early stage. Sex education is the ongoing formation of your child's attitude to their own body, teaching them to respect their own and other people's privacy and teaching them appropriate behaviour.

Finally on the education front, there is your child's spiritual development. The nurture of faith in a small child or even in a growing child is primarily by example. This puts a big responsibility on us. But then that has been the case in all these 'policy' areas such as 'how much TV to watch', 'how much money to spend'. It is our example that shouts the loudest. 'Do as I say, not as I do' simply won't wash. So why should it be any different in the spiritual realm?

Having said that, we do not have to be super saintly to 'succeed'. And we should also bear in mind that each child has their own relationship with God which we cannot dictate or progress by force. We are called to be faithful, obedient and teachable Christians ourselves and to leave the rest up to God. Faithful means we hold on to our faith when the going is tough. Obedient means we live our lives under God's authority just as we expect our kids to live under our authority. Teachable means being willing to admit we're not there yet, we've still got more to learn, we make mistakes.

In spite of our imperfections there is still plenty of scope for encouraging spiritual values. We would do well to make use of such helpful resources such as Bible reading notes and summer camps, if we can. The discovery of the reality of God amongst their own peer group is a very powerful influence on children. If you cannot afford a camp, try arranging for your child to stay with another Christian family so that they discover that theirs is not the only family that goes to church, prays or says grace at meal-times. Offer hospitality to missionaries and widen their vision of the world.

This chapter has been a lightning tour of just some of the responsibilities that go with this stage of motherhood. As you can see, this is not the kind of plate you can simply decide to stop spinning when your children reach a certain age. The challenge is to spin it well at all ages and stages. Even when your children become adults you will still be 'Mum' but your role and style must be continually evolving and changing.

Motherhood is not all nappies, cribs and maternity dresses. I hope that by listing just some of the professional duties of the 'Redcoat' mother, she will have earned a new respect in your eyes. Don't undervalue the power of her position, the potential of her influence or the pressure of her job. This stage of motherhood is perhaps the most over-looked, undervalued and difficult. We find ourselves pulled by pressure from all sides. The pressure to fulfil our home role is perfectly balanced by the pressure to widen our horizons in the world of work.

Chapter 4

The Homemaker

The word 'housewife' has had an undeserved bad press in recent years. It ought to mean 'someone who works in the home but doesn't get paid'. Instead it has come to mean 'someone who doesn't do anything very much'. This is hardly a fair representation of a hardworking individual with a high level of responsibility within the family unit. Several new terms have been coined or revived in an attempt to raise the profile of this key role: household engineer, domestic manager, homemaker or housekeeper. But even these haven't seen off the dowdy image attached to the 'someone' whose chief role is to maintain and run an orderly household.

Homemaking is a very self-effacing job. Everything you do is intended to benefit others. There is no pay, no promotion and the worker receives very little appreciation. It is a physically demanding job, requiring a high degree of organisational skills but it is also boring in parts and often repetitive. If it were the only vocational plate we were called to spin, life might be a great deal easier, if rather dull, but most of us are also called to fulfil the vocation of motherhood and more and more of us also fulfil a professional vocation, or at least take up paid employment outside the home.

In case any of you are labouring under the impression that the emergence of the 'new man' in society has resulted in this role being shared equally between the sexes let me just take a moment to show you the statistics.

In 1984 the British Social Attitudes survey reported that the actual allocation of household tasks in homes inhabited by married couples was:[1]

Washing and ironing	done by the woman	90 per cent of the time
Preparing the evening meal	done by the woman	79 per cent of the time
Cleaning	done by the woman	74 per cent of the time
Sick children	looked after by the woman	64 per cent of the time
Shopping	done by the woman	55 per cent of the time
Handling finances	done by the woman	39 per cent of the time

If you are left still hoping that things have changed in the last decade, the results of my own much more limited survey of Christian households may disillusion you. Here are my statistics for similar tasks:

Washing/ironing/ cleaning	done by the woman	63 per cent of the time
Household shopping	done by the woman	94 per cent of the time
Hospitality	arranged by the woman	90 per cent of the time
Keeping traditions (birthdays, etc.)	arranged by the woman	95 per cent of the time
Finances	arranged by the woman	35 per cent of the time

Although my own survey was a lot less comprehensive it demonstrates clearly that the role of the homemaker is largely left to the female member of a Christian household. My observation was that women whose sole vocations are motherhood and homemaking are better at delegating and sharing chores. Perhaps this is because they have the time to negotiate help whereas those in paid employment may feel, 'It's quicker to do it myself.'

By including such tasks as 'hospitality', and 'keeping traditions', I have tried to demonstrate that 'creating a home' is quite a different thing from 'running a house'. Effective cleaning, shopping and cooking may fill your time and run the household but it falls short of creating a home.

By the end of this chapter I hope we will have discovered how we can be creative homemakers rather than merely efficient housekeepers.

After such depressing statistics it would be good to start our consideration of this role by reminding ourselves of the things we enjoy about it. Out of one hundred returned questionnaires, the most succinct response to the question, 'What do you enjoy about being a homemaker?' was the one-word answer: '*power!*' This sentiment was echoed over and over again by those who said they enjoyed 'being in charge of their own timetable.' This might be a more graceful way to put it but power is what it essentially boils down to. It is a huge advantage to be able to choose what you want to do and when and how you want to do it. To be able to set your own goals and targets without a competitive work environment to contend with, without monthly attainment targets or 'some obnoxious boss breathing down your neck', as one woman put it. All this is true and while it may not compensate for the fact that your home labours are unpaid, it certainly helps.

The next thing that women said they most enjoyed about this role was being able to provide a loving, protective, safe environment for the family. Responses such as these came most often from women who were not in paid employment or only in part-time employment. I suspect that what they mean by this provision has has rather less to do with ironing and cleaning, and rather more to do with creating an atmosphere and being available. One friend of mind who was primarily a homemaker when her children were small said she valued being able to give 'primary socialisation skills to the children'. You can tell she was doing an A-level in psychology at the time. Most of us think of this aspect of home-based life as simply 'being there for the kids'. Or, as another friend of mine put it, rather more realistically, 'The knowledge that the children have a consistent presence in the house, even if she is crabby and bossy.'

After these two beneficial aspects to homemaking, hospitality was easily the most popular with phrases like 'welcoming friends', 'having an open home' and 'making people feel at home' cropping up regularly. The fact that this surprised me tells you more about me than about anyone else. We used to live in a place where hospitality was a cup of coffee, two chocolate digestives and a box of tissues (if needed). I felt I could handle that. Hospitality is not one of my strengths. In fact I may as well confess all now and get it over with: I use gravy granules, I love cook-in sauces, I even make cheesecake from packet mixes. I work on the principle that life is too short to stuff mushrooms, roll chicken breasts or cut carrots into matchsticks. If you, however, really relish that kind of activity then all power to your elbow. For my part, I go for recipes with maximum impact and minimum effort. This frank confession has probably left you relieved that I haven't ever invited you to dinner but if you're anything like me I hope it has comforted you. I have a friend who has the gift of hospitality. She can make a simple coffee morning seem so special and welcoming. I am in awe of the seamless ease with which she welcomes people and serves them simultaneously. I hope I don't leave my guests in any doubt as to my welcome, but those who come regularly know to put the kettle on for themselves.

All of this underlines the fact that we are all made differently and we all have different gifts and preferences. One of my correspondents even liked ironing, not a few others liked gardening and some liked decorating ('when I can do it on my own') and a large number of us liked shopping and cooking (which is just as well given the statistics).

One or two correspondents admitted honestly that nothing appealed to them about the homemaker role and that the only time they enjoyed this role was the few moments between all the work being done and all the work being 'undone' by the rest of the household. So before we get carried away with the positive, wholesome aspects of homemaking, let's bring ourselves back to reality and look at some of the things we don't enjoy about this role.

Far and away the most unpopular chore was household cleaning. It was 'dull', 'repetitive' and 'tedious'. It consumes vast chunks of time and energy and its effects are so short-lived. The same is true of other chores such as washing, cooking or gardening. The dirty linen basket refills just as soon as we have glimpsed the bottom of it. The shelves are emptied shortly after re-stocking, the meals devoured in half the time it took to prepare them and the garden grows defiantly in spite of all our efforts with weedkillers, lawn-mowers and hedge-clippers.

The relentlessness with which the house and garden fall into disorder and chaos can really grind you down. We often talk about 'keeping on top of things' and it can be very disheartening when you feel the house is going to ruin around you. It may, or may not, help you to know that there is a scientific term that describes the situation. The term is 'entropy'. It means 'the measure of disorder in a system'. The second law of thermodynamics involves entropy and states that the direction of any process or system is towards a greater degree of entropy – in other words, things have a tendency to slide into chaos. See, physics is easy! You knew that already. Any homemaker knows that anything left unattended for long will create disorder so why bother with all these scientific terms. They are no good to you at all, except perhaps for impressing any passing teenager who happens to witness your state of collapse on the sofa at the end of the day. You could tell them that you have been testing the second law of thermodynamics and found it to be true.

The other unpopular aspects of the homemaking plate were first the lack of appreciation, promotion or visible achievement and second the problem of always being in your work environment. It is very hard not being able to 'clock in' or 'clock off'. When you live, eat, sleep and celebrate all within the same four walls which you have to scrub, clean, polish or paint, it can be hard to go 'off duty'. One suggestion recommended by several women was to stick to a tea-break and lunch-break routine and have somewhere in the house to which you can retreat and where you can switch off, even if it's just a comfy chair by a window.

So having looked at what we love and what we loathe about being a homemaker, let's get practical and look at a few key tasks in turn.

The Chores

The term 'chores' covers a broad range of activity, including the cleaning, the ironing, the washing and any other repetitive household task. The most common pieces of advice given for these tasks were 'grit your teeth and get on with it, 'get organised', and 'cut every possible corner'. The trouble is we all have different ideas as to what a 'corner' is. A corner for one person may be only hoovering once a week instead of every other day, while someone else may have quite a different attitude to hoovering ('Why find the floor in the first place? When you do you'll only have to hoover it!)

So what most of us do is try to work out what is reasonable. We do this either by measuring ourselves favourably against the standards set by others, or by feeling floored by the expectations others have of us. Either way is unhelpful. My remedy for this situation is summed up in two mottoes and one rule of thumb. The first of the mottoes is this. 'Tidiness is not the tenth fruit of the Spirit' (in spite of what your mother told you). There are virtues that we are called to nurture and value more highly: love, joy, peace, patience, kindness, goodness, faithfulness, gentleness, and self-control (Gal. 5:22). The second motto is one I found on a little wall plaque. It says, 'Dull women have immaculate houses.' I used to display this text defiantly by the front door but, as it is rather offensive to well-organised, tidy' types, I have now hidden it away beside my desk where it secretly refuels me if I'm feeling drained by my failings as a 'housewife'. It contains the same grain of truth as the first motto, which is that there are rather more important things in life to strive for than an immaculate home.

My rule of thumb regarding housework deals with the problem of other people's standards, as well as giving you a level to aim at. It is simply this. *'Live in an environment which you control, not an environment which controls you.'* This rule works for my friend who can't see her carpets. By some people's standards her home is untidy (putting it mildly), but as she has a high tolerance for disorder she feels herself to be in control. The same rule works for the person for whom a daily once-over round the house is all that is required to feel in control. For me a weekly 'blitz' is all I can bear. It's the grumpiest hour of the week and countless people have told me it would be quicker and easier to do a little every day but I simply want to live in my house for six days a week. I don't want to clean it, so I settle for a weekly 'blitz'. The only other time I tidy is when I can't face whatever it is I'm really meant to be doing. It beats chewing the end of a pencil. So if you visit my home and it's immaculate you'll know that I've been having a very unproductive week at my desk.

It is totally inappropriate for me to dictate standards to other people just as it would be unwise for me to judge people by the appearance of their home. As far as I'm concerned the only criteria by which I can decide 'Am I doing okay?' is whether or not I feel in control. I've developed this standard because over the years I've noticed that whenever I feel out of control in my home environment that feeling of disorder and discouragement quickly extends to the rest of my life. If I don't feel on top of things the statement, 'The house is in a mess' can easily mean the same thing as 'My whole life is in a mess.' If you spend most of your time in your home it can easily become a metaphor for your life.

This idea has been captured very effectively in the following poem by Adrian Plass.[2] He writes as someone engaged in that most depressing of tasks: writing the list of things to be done.

Once I've cleaned this house up properly,
I honestly think I'll get somewhere.
Once I've pulled out every single piece of furniture and
    used an abrasive cloth with strong stuff on it,
I think I shall come to terms with the rest of my life.
Once I've put everything into separate piles, each
    containing the same sort of thing (if you know what I
    mean)
I think I'll manage.
Once I've written a list that includes absolutely
    everything,
I think the whole business will seem much clearer.
Once I've had time to work slowly from one item to
    another,
I'm sure things will change.
Once I've eaten sensibly for more than a week and a
    half,
Once I've sorted out the things that are my fault,
Once I've spent a little more time reading useful books,
Being with people I like,
Going to pottery classes,
Getting out into the air,
Making bread,
Drinking less,
Drinking more,
Going to the theatre,
Adopting a third world child,
Eating free range eggs,
And writing long letters,
Once I've pulled every single piece of furniture *right out*,
And cleaned this house up properly,
Once I've become someone else . . .
I honestly think I'll get somewhere.

We often become so overwhelmed by what we have to do
and what we want to do that we end up feeling like a failure
on all fronts. Housework surely comes into the first category

of things that 'have to be done' so let's simply do the minimum and get it over with. One of my correspondents noticed that housework will expand to fill the time allocated to it, so she suggested the obvious: allocate it a limited time. There are so many more important things to be done from the 'things we want to do list' that it's pointless to let the urgent squeeze out the important.

Housework ought to carry a 'health warning' as it can be addictive and can make people obsessional. I speak from experience. I was recently loaned one of those 'how to do everything successfully' manuals. This one was about how to clean your home in thirty seconds a day. It was an engrossing read. I lay awake at night plotting the reform of my cleaning methods. It led to a large financial outlay purchasing new plastic bowls, squeegees and spray bottles. I read that 70 per cent of my household goods could be classified as 'junk'. According to this cleaning guru, in the average household we only ever use 30 per cent of the things we possess. We live in a small house so this statistic really grabbed me. The thought of reducing the amount of 'stuff' I have to tidy, sort and clean by 70 per cent really appealed to me. I ordered a skip!

For one rash and intense week I progressively 'de-junked' the whole house. The contents of every cupboard and shelf were emptied, thinned out and re-loaded. I became totally obsessed with clear work surfaces and orderly cupboards. I became addicted to filling bin bags and rather more importantly I became grumpy, irritable and totally exhausted. My daily quiet time became a 'list of chores to do today' session and my inner life shrivelled up. I think it was when my 'clean sweep' reached the under-stairs cupboard that I finally found myself on my knees. This could have been mistaken for a saintly posture were it not for the fact that I was in the dark surrounded by Wellington boots and hoover attachments, clutching a torch in one hand and a bin bag in the other, In this unlikely situation I felt a verse being divinely nudged into my mind. 'What good will it be for a man if he

gains the whole world, yet forfeits his soul?' (Matt. 16:26).
Aware of my recent scant attention to God's word I mulled
this over for a few minutes not really making any sense of
it. As I did so, it slowly reformulated itself until the message
was loud and clear.

'What good will it be for a woman if she has the cleanest,
most orderly home at the expense of her spiritual or home
life?'

That was the last cupboard I went through!

If you are ever tempted to get obsessional about housework to the point of being ratty with the kids or aggressive
with your husband then a reassessment of priorities might
be in order.

So having taken a long time to tell you that housework is
not the be-all and end-all in life, here are the 'pick and mix'
selection of tips to pass on from my correspondents about
how to be 'in control' of your home. I include the contradic-
tions because I find them an entertaining reminder that we
are all different.

- Pay someone else to do the chores.
- Involve the rest of the family.
- Use a list. It gives you a feeling of achievement.
- Abandon lists. They'll only depress you.
- Clean a little every day, early in the day if possible.
- Do the ironing while watching the TV or listening to the radio.
- Pay a teenager to iron *or* give whoever is prepared to use the iron the right to control the TV remote.
- Don't do any one job for too long.
- Do each job thoroughly until it is done.
- Keep one room presentable and allow for a decrease in presentability in proportion to the likehihood of the room being seen.
- Clean with a friend who likes housework (if you can find such a rare individual).
- Have a 'system' for anything and everything. A system is

a planned strategy for any task you dislike. 'Ignore it', 'do it on Saturdays' or 'only buy blue ones' are all versions of workable systems related to window cleaning, shopping and the pairing up of children's socks! A system should free up that part of your mind that you would otherwise have to devote to organising the task in hand. A good system requires minimum time and energy to run. Colour-coded baskets for dirty/crumpled/clean clothes is an example of a laundry system.

● And finally, if all other motivation fails you, reward yourself with chocolate (this from a chocoholic friend).

In conclusion, it seems that there are only two things to be done about this unattractive aspect of homemaking. You can either change the chores or change your attitude. It is possible to cut down on the former and smarten up the latter. Screaming, shouting and being unreasonable will feel good but it won't get you anywhere. On the other hand, choosing to serve your family in the mundane tasks of life can become a positive choice. Possibly it is even part of every Christian's calling to self-denial or 'picking up your cross daily'. When the mundaneness and repetitiveness of it all gets me down I read this thought by Pamela Reeve:

God is the God of *now* carrying on his purpose in every tedious, dull, stupid, boring, empty minute of my life.[3]

Seemingly meaningless tasks can be given value and meaning if you know your own value and calling as a servant in God's household.

The Shopping

This isn't as loathed a task as 'the chores' but there are still plenty of helpful ways in which it can be streamlined.

- Cash tills are like taximeters: the more often you shop and the longer you are in the shop the greater the final bill, so shop as infrequently as possible.
- Use a weekly menu or a list of regularly acceptable meals.
- Use a freezer.
- Use a good catalogue for clothes and other goods if you can't bear trawling round the shops.
- If you shop for specific items it will save you time and money but on the other hand some of the best buys are things you 'just happen to see'. Keep a box or cupboard for the hoarding of 'good buys' for Christmas or birthdays. It helps spread the cost.
- Supermarket shopping can be done in half the time if you try 'trolley races': each parent gets half of the shopping list with half of the siblings and the last one to finish buys the doughnuts in the café.
- And finally, did you know that people who have credit cards spend, on average, 35 per cent more than people who don't? Sobering thought.

One suggestion that was made several times over was, 'Keep raising the expectations of how much the children will do around the house as they grow older.' For as many women who made this suggestion an equal number beamoaned the impossibility of putting it into effect. If you are going to *delegate* chores you have first of all to slow down and *demonstrate* how chores are done and then stand back and enthuse over their inept, but well-meant, efforts. It is often so much simpler to do it ourselves.

Tidy children are a rarity, but they do exist. I know because I have one. Before you ask, no, she is not available for hire or loan. Nor is her tidiness tendency always the asset you might think. When she rises early on a Saturday, sorts her own room out, puts out her younger brother's clothes, then makes moves on your room whilst you are still firmly ensconced in it, you come to appreciate the drawbacks of having a small person around whose standards are higher than yours. At one time her 'ideal' way to spend a Saturday would have been to tidy the house in the morning and the garden in the afternoon. She loves to wake up to a 'list of things to do today'. Her list will include items such as 'Hoover room', 'rearrange fridge magnets', 'tidy desk' (hers). She will not appear for breakfast until she reaches the 'eat breakfast' item on her list.

I have particularly vivid memories of the morning she decided to lay the breakfast bar in the kitchen. We had 'silver service' for what is usually a 'one star, fix-it-yourself' affair. The cups, bowls, plates, knives, spoons plus the entire contents of the cereal cupboard were laid out on the kitchen surfaces. While she had executed this feat of helpfulness the rest of us had overslept. This meant that all four of us had twenty minutes to eat and dress and one of us (me) had twenty minutes to eat, dress and fill the lunch boxes.

Having placated her with what appeared to be an acceptable amount of appreciative noises, we charged through breakfast. Once through eating, the dressing began upstairs, while I did the lunch boxes. Needing to finish this task with at least two minutes spare in which I could get dressed, I was making fairly good headway until I came across the last two yoghurts in the fridge. They were the kind contained in plastic pots that are meant to snap apart and as they were required in two separate places I proceeded to 'snap' them. However, these two were inseparable. Needless to say no scissors were to be found in any of the preordained places for scissors to be kept so I was left with the unenviable task of sawing apart two yoghurt pots with a carving knife. This was not very successful and so five minutes later, having at least managed to dress, I stormed out of the house leaving a trail of spilt yoghurt all over the kitchen and ranting rabidly about buying the first half dozen pairs of scissors I found and hanging one from a string in the corner of each room and then maybe they wouldn't 'just disappear'.

I digress, but as lunch boxes are a particular pet hate of mine I can't bring myself to omit a word about them.

Lunch Boxes

First you have to fill lunch boxes with something that
especially appeals to your particular child. This something
has to reach some basic standard of nutrition, be easy to
obtain and require minimum preparation (stuffed peppers
'out', peanut butter sandwiches 'in'). The rush and hassle of
filling the box is merely half the chore. By late afternoon
you find, returned to your kitchen table, the 'empty' lunch
box. If only it were empty it wouldn't be so bad. In fact it is
full of mandarin peel mixed up with yoghurt and limp crisps
soaked in squash. This concoction has been sitting around
for at least three hours getting warm and smelly. If you
could simply open the lid and ditch the contents that would
help but first you have to fish around for the spoon.
Somewhere in there, usually bonded to the kitchen towel
'serviette', is the spoon you gave them for their yoghurt.
This morning it was fresh out of the dishwasher. Now it is
caked with the yoghurt-crisp-squash mixture. There is little
that can be done to alleviate the chore of the lunch box but
here are one or two suggestions.

- Send your children for school dinners. You're not just paying for the meal, you are paying for a hassle-free morning.
- Don't give them yoghurt until at least Wednesday at the
  earliest. That way you may be able to ignore the stains
  down the jumper till Friday.
- Don't send in anything that can melt, spill or explode
  during the three hours between delivery to school and
  lunchtime. (Note: fizzy drinks in Tupperware containers
  explode. This is a mistake you make only once.)
- Pack the lunch boxes the night before, or prepare contents
  and put them in the fridge, or have ready-frozen packs of
  sandwiches.
- Once the children reach the age of about eight, they can
  pack their own.

So much for the efficient housekeeping suggestions. What about creative homemaking? As the difference between a home and a house centres on the presence of a family, it ought to be clear that the ways to be a homemaker and not merely a housekeeper centre around ways to keep the family functioning as a 'well-oiled' unit. Here are a few hints in this direction.

Keeping Traditions

Children love to look forward to enjoyable events such as Christmas and their birthday. These occasions have to be reliably enjoyable. The birthday routine may become very predictable but most children prefer it that way. It doesn't take much to establish a tradition. You do something a certain way one year and the children expect the experience to be repeated the next.

'So all my presents will be piled up on your dressing-table like last year,' my over-excited six-year-old said on the eve of her seventh birthday. I'd probably only piled them up on there to save me having to go very far early in the morning, but a simple tradition had been started. Another family I know have the rule that you can eat whatever you want for breakfast on Christmas morning (this invariably means the consumption of huge quantities of chocolate). 'Tradition' may sound like a rather grand word but I simply mean the funny little foibles that make your family unique. We have a set of different coloured flags, one for each member of the family. These are small enough to live in a vase in the front room but bright enough to use as a table decoration on the tea table. So whenever someone has done anything remotely outstanding or noteworthy we put their flag out for them.

Filling Memory Banks

We all of us have a store of memories from our own childhood locked away somewhere in our subconscious mind. Some memories we can recall: happy times, sad times, seemingly insignificant snapshots or hugely detailed recollections. Other memories lie beyond our conscious reach but their influence can still seep silently into all we do. We stocked the shelves of our memory banks from whatever material was available.

I'm not an expert but it seems to me that younger children seem to store the atmosphere of the home rather than the specifics of experience. So you cannot insist that your three-year-old remember the birthday cake you slaved over for hours, nor must you be disappointed if that hugely expensive day out never made it on to the recall shelf. I had a widely exciting life before I was seven. I lived in four different continents, survived civil unrest, walked unaided up a glacier and toured Japan. How much of this enriching experience can I remember? Not a jot! I recall my nursery teacher's fat legs (but not her face), the pattern on a favourite anorak and some pictures on a wall which frightened me.

While it is somewhat disappointing that all this foreign travel was wasted on me, it is more remarkable that I have no recollection of ever feeling unsettled by this lifestyle. So it's worth remembering that although children will store away some bad memories, if we provide them with enough material some good ones will also be stored.

Holidays, happy days, Saturdays and birthdays are all great days for making memories by doing something daft and unexpected together. It doesn't have to involve expense although when expense is incurred it helps to remind ourselves that it is easy to scrimp a few pennies into the savings bank but it takes a little extra to invest in a memory bank. If the perfect thing that would round off the day (almost always a cream tea in my case), costs a little more, it is sometimes worth it.

Finding Family Time

It might seem odd to finish this chapter with a section on 'Finding Family Time' when you'd expect a homemaker to be totally immersed in the needs of the home and family. However, it is possible for most of our time in the home to be taken up with moving things from here to there (otherwise known as tidying), cooking, washing plates or sorting clothes. Unless we are aware that these jobs will expand to fill however much time we allocate to them they will take over all our time and squeeze out opportunities for the family to talk, listen, laugh, and generally 'eyeball' each other.

We have found it helpful to have a designated time in the week that is known as 'family time'. This not-so-snappy title is at least self-explanatory. Family time for us happens on a Thursday after tea. It might sound a bit artificial but I challenge you to see how often you deliberately set aside time to talk together if you are working on the assumption that 'It'll happen sometime.' Even with a system in place it quite often gets squeezed out. We are a very ordinary, busy family, so family time often gets overlooked for a week or two but now that it's become part of the rhythm of family life the children will often remind us, 'It's Thursday, Mum. What are we doing for family time?' It only takes ten minutes and a little forethought.

We began when our children were three and five with seasonal activities such as leaf rubbing in autumn or making multicoloured pancakes for Pancake day. When it was Valentine's day we each had a cardboard heart on which we wrote or drew the things we liked best about the other members of the family. A press-out cardboard model of Noah's Ark took six weeks to complete. Only once have we been totally silly and picked Smarties out of flour mounds with our teeth but they haven't forgotten that one! Other things you can do would be to listen to stories, resolve a few problems or plan special events. I first heard the idea recommended for older children who would benefit from the brain-storming and problem-solving techniques more common in committees than in families, we haven't done much of that yet but at least with the time set aside there is the opportunity for it.

These final three suggestions can become the planks that strengthen the foundation of family life, so console yourself when the wash basket is overflowing and the floor hasn't been seen for weeks, being a happy homemaker is better than being a harassed housekeeper, any day.

Chapter 5

The Clockwork Mummy

'When is a working mother a working mother?' No, it's not a joke, nor is it meant to be a trick question, but if you think about it for a moment you will realise it is not such an easy question to answer.

Is a 'working mother' one whose labour is recognised by a contract and who receives a pay-packet at the end of the month? Or is a 'working mother' one whose chief labour is the full-time fulfilment of her vocation as mother? Surely both of these women are in a full-time occupation, in which case, aren't all mothers 'working mothers'?

We have just spent three chapters exploring the vocations of motherhood and homemaker. These vocations require work; work that is invariably unpaid. So as we turn our attention to the world of paid employment I think it would be helpful to abandon the notion that only women who get paid, work hard. To do this we need to get rid of the misleading and much maligned phrase, 'working mother'.

The title of this chapter is my attempt at a sympathetic replacement. 'Clockwork' is a tribute to women in paid employment because it carries overtones of efficiency and predictable punctuality; all desirable personal qualities for anyone seeking to sign a job contract. But 'clockwork' also has realistic overtones of inflexible regularity, and of the sort of self-discipline that has to disregard feelings (I'd rather be on the beach) and circumstances (Katie's got a cold ... again'). Clockwork Mummies need to have these sorts of qualities and tend to experience these sorts of problems. Not only do they have to 'clock in' and out of work; they also have to clock-watch all through breakfast, through the rush hour traffic to the school gate, through the working hours, through the supermarket queue, back through the evening traffic and all through the 'collect, cook, clean and get ready for the next day' routine. Little wonder then that by late evening, when the clock work winds down, the Clockwork Mummy is to be found curled up in a chair able to do little more than stare through the steam of a comforting cup of tea.

Mothers who are in paid employment are an indisputable fact of modern life. In 1994 53 per cent of women were in paid employment.[1] In the Eighties there was a certain amount of pressure on feminist-minded mothers to return to work full-time in order to show that having children did not interfere with women's ability to equal men. It is unlikely that this pressure completely accounts for the increase in women in paid employment, of which the percentage rose from 44 per cent in 1971. This rise is more likely due to the increased availability of part-time work and women's preference for it. In 1995, the Central Statistical Office's survey on women reported that 92 per cent of women married with children said they did not want a full-time job. Part-time work is now a positive choice made by more and more women once they have had children.

It seems to me that the reason for this partly lies in the different ways that men and women perceive the spheres of home and work. For a man, work and home are two opposite environments. The former is a place of often competitive labour and the latter is a place for rest and relaxation. For a woman, home and work are environments that may compete for her attention but they are not necessarily so separately defined. Home is often synonymous with work (especially if the statistics about who does the housework are to be believed) and 'work', that is, paid employment, is often linked to fulfilment.

I know that there are exceptions to this way of looking at life – for example in the case of couples who have reversed roles, or who balance work and child care between them –

but in my experience the situation in which the man has a full-time career and the woman has a part-time 'interest' is far more common. I'm not about to judge whether this is right or wrong. It is simply an observation to bear in mind as we come to consider the 'career spinning plate': women in the working world.

Does all this part-time work actually leave women better off? By working part-time haven't they just added yet another plate to their already complicated plate-spinning act? Part-time is often a poor deal financially, so can women really 'have it all'? Is it possible to be a successful mother and cultivate creative employment opportunities? Is work simply a grinding economic necessity or can it enhance family life? Or is child-rearing totally incompatible with career development?

These are all very personal questions with which many of us have struggled. There is no neat answer that is universally applicable. Each of us has to consider our own situation very seriously. We weigh up the needs of our children, our own desires and expectations, the needs of the family and, if we are Christians, we are also called to listen for God's call on our life. It is this final factor that should be the determining one. Several women told me that their return to employment had been 'because God opened the door', but a similar number felt equally called to unpaid labour in the home. This doesn't mean some of us are hearing God right and some of us are hearing him wrong; it is simply a demonstration of the fact that God deals with us as individuals. But it can be hard to hear God's voice for ourselves. In the secular world, few would challenge our choice to work outside the home but in the Christian community there are many strongly held opinions and conflicting expectations that can leave us tied up in knots of guilt and confusion. It can be very difficult to discern what God is really calling us to do.

In the days when equal educational opportunities were not available, women had little choice. Now that the choice exists the responsibility to choose wisely is greatly increased. This issue was brought into focus for me when I took my own six-year-old daughter for a walk around my old university campus. Explaining to her that this was where I had lived and studied, and defining such difficult terms as 'qualifications' and 'degrees', I managed to get across the fact that Mummy had only been able to become a teacher because she had come and studied here first. I was hoping she'd look impressed. Instead a rather worried expression flickered across her face. I had hoped that the visit would have put 'further education' high on her list of desirable life experiences so I was concerned about the worried look. Seeking to allay her fears, I asked if she had any questions.

'Yes,' she promptly replied. 'Do I need "qualifitations" to be a mummy, because that's what I want to be when I grow up?'

This was no simple question. What should I have said? If I'd opted for the straightforward 'You don't need qualifications to be a mummy', I would have undermined the value of further education and the requirements for motherhood in a single sentence. Perhaps I should have said, 'Well, being a mummy usually comes after being something else', thus relegating motherhood to being a secondary vocation? I could even have said, 'You need to be something before you become a mummy' but thankfully I didn't, as that would have implied that being a mummy was the equivalent of being a nothing. How could I reply in a way that would help my daughter hold the prospect of motherhood in balance with all the rest of life's opportunities?

In the end, after a long stall, I muttered something limp about university being great fun and 'You'll feel differently about it when you get older'. I didn't answer the real issue she had raised. Perhaps at six she was too young to comprehend a dilemma that I still find myself tussling with at times. The problem in a nutshell is, for all women who have a career and children, how do we justify two vocations? Even if we can justify them, can we do justice to motherhood and a career? Perhaps, like me, you believe that motherhood is a high, God-given calling, and that an effective mother is a powerful force for good in society. Do you also believe that mothers are creative, valuable members of society who have a legitimate part to play in the marketplace, in schools, in local government, in the health system, in fact in any place where men are allowed to use their skills?

I passionately believe both of these statements but it is not easy holding them in balance when it comes to putting one's theory into practice. As one cartoonist put it, 'Balancing a job and a family is not the hardest thing to achieve. It's the second . . . right after world peace.' Does that mean to say it should not be attempted just because it is hard? Some people would say, 'Yes, women and children both lose out when mothers attempt to hold down paid employment.' While this may be the case for some families, it is not necessarily true for all. In particular it is not true for those families where employment for the mother is essential for the family's economic survival. Other people would say, 'No, women should not shelve their skills and stifle their frustration. If paid employment leaves them personally fulfilled, or better off, then family life is enhanced all round.' Some women can find personal fulfilment in full-time motherhood but others, whose skills lie outside of the sphere of child care, can suffer condemnation from a Christian subculture that has elevated motherhood to the status of a supreme calling for all married women.

While so many conflicting opinions exist, the only thing that is clear is that if you are going to attempt something universally acknowledged to be difficult, it is very important that you have a clear idea about why you are doing it. Even if you feel that it is not a matter of personal choice (you 'have to' work) it is still preferable for you to have thought through the whys and wherefore of paid employment. That way you may be able to work without an unnecessary sense of guilt.

So, Why Work?

My own reasons are that I want my children to see that motherhood has enriched and enhanced my life. I hope the evidence for this is obvious, in that I make it clear I enjoy being a mum. It is a responsibility I have embraced, not a burden I've had to put up with. I also want them to see that I am a person apart from being a mother. I have gifts, skills and interests that are not related to them. I have a part to play in the wider world and my life is not totally bound up with theirs. The period of their dependency on me is not likely to be as long as my working life, and while I may have invested several years into their nurture and establishment, like a river diverting its course and shaping part of the landscape in the process, I must eventually flow on in my own direction. For me this meant being out of regular paid employment for a period of five or six years. For others the break from paid work may be shorter or much longer but that is their individual choice.

Many of us try to keep these two dimensions of our lives – home and work – in balance but we are often made to feel that we just can't win. Workplace practices or the demands of a profession can make part-time flexibility almost an impossibility. As if that weren't enough, the attitudes of others can be hard to swallow. 'Why did she have kids if she really wanted to work?' or 'She just can't cope at home, that's why she works', or the flattery to her face: 'I don't know *how* you do it' that hides the unspoken criticism of your Christian commitment: 'Of course, she's too busy now to help out with the church cleaning.'

This isn't meant to be a criticism of those who do dedicate their time and energy to voluntary activities such as church cleaning. Such tasks are very worthwhile in themselves, but for anyone trying to balance their need/desire to be in paid employment with all the rest of life's demands it is easy to feel paranoid and frustrated. Paranoid, because you can't please everyone and so there will always be people who will find something to complain about. Frustrated, because men don't face this dilemma. It is apparently okay for men to procreate *and* fulfil their career ambitions. Why is this? If motherhood is a 'high calling' surely fatherhood is of equal value? Why is it that when a newspaper survey discovered that one in three of the labour force are 'women with family responsibilities' they didn't even bother to ask what proportion of working men had 'family responsibilities'? Surely it is because a woman's family responsibilities are assumed to affect her work and invade her life in a way that a man's responsibilities are not. Until this failure to recognise the role and responsibility of fatherhood is eradicated, men will continue to have to work in an environment that excludes their families or assumes that they take second place.

Instead of discouraging women from the workplace, perhaps Christians should focus more attention on the need to discourage the working practices that encourage men to be 'workaholics' and put their career development above everything else. It is very hard for a man to determine that he will not give this job more than 'the pound of flesh' the contract requires. If the job is seen to take second place to his home and family relationships, he is perceived as lacking ambition and commitment. Because of this pressure on men, women are under an unequal pressure to 'keep the home fires burning'. This is the reason why I lie awake at night listening to a coughing child and worrying about another day's labour lost or 'What arrangements can I make this time?' while my husband lies next to me snoring contentedly in the knowledge that in the morning he can go off to work 'come hell or high water' at home. This isn't just because he earns more than I do, nor because my job is more flexible than his, although both are true. It is principally because the children's needs and demands invade my life far more than they invade his. This 'fact of life' may be part of the God-given role of motherhood or it may be imposed on us by society; whichever is true it remains a powerful dynamic in most women's lives.

So then, given that the children do need me and are occasionally sick, why do I bother to work at all? This was one of the questions I put to the women who completed my questionnaire: what are your reasons for either being in paid employment or not? Most of the women were Christians yet the percentage of those doing some paid employment was close to the national average of 53 per cent. (So if Christian mothers are not meant to work, over half of us are in rebellion.) The main reason for not having a paid job was 'personal choice', usually related to the fact that they had small children at home. Several pointed out that this 'personal choice' was available to them because they could manage financially on one salary. One or two said they couldn't find appropriate part-time work in the area of their ability and another complained that child care costs would eat up most of her potential earnings anyway.

The main reasons given for going out to work were the same: 'personal choice' and 'financial need'. They were usually given together. Explaining their personal choice to work, women said things like 'I needed a place to be me', 'to keep me sane', 'to see if I had a brain', 'a badly needed outlet', 'a mental challenge', 'to use all my skills' and 'for personal fulfilment'. Are these reasons the self-centred murmurings of a group of badly behaved mothers who don't seem to find sufficient meaning in motherhood alone? I don't think so. Personally I think these are all very valid reasons for returning to work and they are not necessarily self-centred. What is good for the mother is often, by extension, good for the family. One woman wrote, 'It renewed my love for my son.' Another said, 'The child care created an extended family for my child.' My own experience was that my two-year-old and I got on decidedly better for having spent a few hours apart. A sane mother is a better mother than the one who is sticking it out at home 'for the sake of the kids' and loathing every minute of it.

It is a great shame that certain well-known Christians should have spoken recently in a way that appears to condemn mothers who work. One such remark was to the effect that 'women only work for status and money'. To which my reply would be, 'Yes, and what's wrong with status and money?' When God created employment these were the two blessings that he had in mind for both of his workers: male and female. It is God's intention that we should have a meaningful existence that maintains us. The fact that employment confers self-respect is a God-given equation. It is the reason why unemployment and redundancy are such an assault on human dignity. Why should the stimulation, accountability, salary and status of a job be a stigma for Christian women when it was what God intended work to confer on all human beings?

For many families, the father's job is not as secure as it was in previous generations, nor is life as simple. The women in my survey who worked because of financial need were doing simply that, not working from financial greed. Their money was paying bills and putting food on the table in just the same way as their husband's income was covering the rent or mortgage or keeping the car on the road. The bias against women working is a strong middle-class hangover. If you have ever lived in a working-class area you will find that they have no such prejudice against women working. The husband will come off one shift as the wife goes out to another. Women staying at home all day is a cultural notion that goes along with the nine-to-five mentality. It is also a middle-class belief that meaning and purpose is to be found uniquely in the unpaid raising of children. It comes down to us from the Fifties with a picture of a little woman at home making apple pie.

I've got nothing against apple pie, nor against women who do choose the unpaid labour of full-time child care. Having chosen this vocation myself for several years, I would campaign for their cause to be better supported by law and their status to be recognised, but at the same time I would appeal for freedom of choice. This is not the only mould for all mothers. There are several other moulds which are also biblical.

The women's liberation movement has done a lot to break up the 'little woman at home' mould, but it has only replaced it with other 'moulds'. There is the 'I don't need a man to complement me' mould which results in the politically single; or there is the 'career mother' mould which has resulted in the style of mothering where the children do not appear to have had any impact on their mother's life. Not only have they failed to divert her career, they haven't even ruffled her hair or thickened her waistline!

The only way through this minefield of expectations and opinions is to throw away all these moulds and be your own woman. Paul wrote in his letter to the Romans: 'Do not conform . . . to the pattern of this world, but be transformed . . .' (Rom. 12:2) In other words, don't be one thing or the other just because you think that is what is expected of you. Break the mould. Be what God created you to be and follow his direction. This means respecting the fact that God's direction may lead other women to make different choices. It is up to us to get our cue from God, not from the cultural norm of our church community or from the society around us. After all, the good wife of Proverbs 31 probably wouldn't fit into our current cultural norms. She is one of the biblical moulds I mentioned earlier. She bought and sold. She worked the late shift into the night. She grew a vineyard out of her own income. (I wonder how *my* husband would react if I ploughed my income into a home-brewing venture!) She employed other people and struck deals with tradesmen. If she were to turn up in your church, would she raise a few eyebrows? Can you hear the remarks now? 'A busy, bossy woman.' 'Out for all she can get.' 'Obviously got some axe to grind.' But, thankfully, there she is in the Bible held up as a paragon of female virtue, we'd do well to remember her.

If there is such a thing as an 'ideal woman' mould, the

lady in Proverbs 31 ought to come close. But as we model ourselves on her in our modern world, we will each come up with our own interpretation of her faithful industrious. To do so, we must reject the 'ideal woman' mould foisted on us by glossy magazines. You know the kind of woman I mean: two 'glowing with health' children, a perfect complexion, an immaculate home, a size twelve figure, a flatteringly female type of job and a nippy little 'run around'. This woman is a figment of the advertising industry's imagination. You must not let her intimidate you, she does not exist very often. Moreover, let me say loudly for one last time, before I get off my soap box, women can find fulfilment in a huge variety of different lifestyles, different job descriptions and different dress sizes.

Full-Time or Part-Time?

Now we've thrashed out the theory let's turn our attention to the practical issues involved with spinning the paid employment plate. Out of all my correspondents, fifty-one (a little over half) were in part-time jobs. Only nine worked full-time. Of these, three were either missionaries or in full-time ministry training. Only two had small children still at home; one of these worked from home and the other was a teacher. The other six all had children over the age of ten. The fact that so few do work full-time is not automatically evidence that 'it ought not to be done', but rather is evidence of first, how hard it is to do and second, that many of us are happy for the motherhood plate to temper our career spinning style. The part-time/full-time issue might also depend on the age of your children and certainly on your marital status.

Undoubtedly, working full time places work very high on the agenda. If you don't want to place it so high on your agenda but you do want to keep your skills up to date or have some employment outlet then part-time work seems ideal. As many have found it also has its drawbacks. First, there is the problem of how you are perceived at work. 'Half-time, half-committed, half-there and half-witted' was one lady GP's poetical expression. The notion that you are not really committed to your job or that you are just in it 'for the pocket money' can be very hard for women to overcome. Added to this is the fact that their opinions are often not taken seriously. They have less muscle when it comes to negotiating pay and conditions so they are often not as well-paid as their full-time counterparts, nor are their pension benefits and rights as great.

Second, there are the practical problems that paid employment generates for a mother. A part-time job carries the same problems as a full-time job – for example, child care and juggling the home life – simply to a lesser degree. So a part-time job can still feel like a full-time preoccupation and, in the case of a job share, each half-timer may work for longer than they are paid, to ensure a smooth changeover. If you are not yet a Clockwork Mummy, don't let the following list of potential problems put you off. They have to be faced realistically but don't despair, at least not until you have reached the list of practical suggestions. If you are already a Clockwork Mummy, you may feel comforted by the fact that other mums face the same dilemmas. Their first three problems were a variation on the same theme:

- The number one problem is child care. Those best placed in the child care stakes were mothers who had helpful extended family nearby, or those able to employ friends as childminders (although one or two felt this complicated a friendship).
- The second biggest problem was also child care – this time child care for the school holidays. Term-time employment is a distinct advantage if you can get it.
- The third biggest problem was – surprise, surprise – child care again. What do you do when the children are ill? One woman wisely remarked that the fear of spots at 7

a.m. has always been larger than life. The imaginary
scenario of 'ailing child and departing mother' is not
usually so bad in reality.

- Other problems were (in no particular order): the tendency for work to escalate, deadlines, extra stress, tiredness, and guilt, guilt and more guilt. Self-imposed,
inflicted by others, you name it, they'd felt it. Guilt is a
big issue.

Before we drown in a sea of guilt and despair, let's move
quickly on to the practical suggestions that may make this
plate spin smoothly. They may be a few in number but as
there was such universal agreement about them from my
correspondents I'm sure they are valuable:

- Get organised. Allocate your time to the various tasks in
hand: paid labour, leisure, unpaid labour. If possible, pay
someone else to do any tasks that you do not have to do
yourself.
- Marry a flexible spouse. This piece of forward planning
may come a little late in the day for some of us but it
draws attention to the fact that the school holidays and
what to do with sick kids problem can be a lot easier if
your spouse is able to take time off or work flexibly. He
also needs to be totally interchangeable with you so that
anything you would do in the home he can do.
- If your husband can't help, several flexible friends are
vital (not the plastic variety). Have a shortlist of friends
and neighbours who could help you out at short notice to
collect after school or have a 'slightly under the weather'
child for you. This list works better as a network. In other
words, the help you receive from your friends is mutual.
When they are in need you will return the favour. This
list does not replace your regular child care arrangements,
it's only for emergency cover.
- Be prepared to do extensive research to find the type of
child care that suits you and your children: a nanny, a

childminder, an after-school club, a private nursery, an au pair. Peace of mind is worth paying for. Ask questions about anything and everything to do with the care on offer. Make clear your expectations and requirements from the outset. (For more advice on looking for child care try your library for recently published handbooks for working mothers, lists of childminders and details of nurseries.)

- Be pro-active in your search for work. Only settle for the hours you feel you can handle. In order to do this, you must first make an accurate assessment of what you can do/want to do. Short-term contracts can help in this regard allowing you frequently to review the situation but they score zero in terms of security or forward planning.
- Work whole-heartedly and play whole-heartedly.
- Work locally if possible. Why spend child care time, for which you are paying, stuck in a traffic jam?
- Don't work too close to home. A delightful contradiction of the previous statement! Perhaps the issue is not really about geography but about keeping home and work distinct. This is very hard to do if you work from home. Women who work from home need to publicise their working hours to the rest of the world and have the self-discipline to walk past the laundry basket and dirty dishes straight to their desk/work-bench (not a problem for some of us).
- Write things down. This can include everything from the trivial observations about the contents of the fridge to your concerns about your child; also any bright ideas you have about how to rearrange the home or what to buy your mother for Christmas. There are few more tedious experiences than knowing you filed an important piece of information somewhere in your mind and being totally unable to recall it. Pots of cheap biros and scraps of paper are my most vital home accessory.
- Have a morning routine and a 'return from work/school' routine. If everyone knows in advance who fixes breakfast or empties the dishwasher, if the dinner money and school

bags are always put in the same place, then the possibility of a smooth running morning are increased. These routines aren't petty if they help everyone go their separate ways in the morning like civilised human beings. A frenzy of lost keys, frayed tempers and banged doors can leave you with a feeling of disturbance that can last all day. Similarly a 'decompression routine' for when everyone gets in from work and/or school can help everyone readjust to being together again. A few minutes spent chatting over a drink and a biscuit is often better than rushing to get the dinner on straight away.

- Handling stress. Advice in this area varied from 'eat well', 'take exercise and see good friends often', to 'avoid alcohol' and 'breathe through alternate nostrils'! (I don't know quite how this is supposed to help but it conjures up a wonderful vision of stressed supermarket shoppers, standing in queues, holding their noses and breathing deeply to maintain their inner equilibrium!) Obviously, it is sensible to take care of yourself. You cannot expect your body or your emotions to cope with greater demands unless you provide them with enough fuel and replenishment. The evidence is that women are suffering from increased anxiety and stress and are drinking more.[2] If these pitfalls are to be avoided you need to watch the gauges on your personal resources of physical, emotional and spiritual energy.

Guilt is one emotion that drains personal resources quickly. I could have written a section on guilt for each and every one of the 'plates' we have looked at. It was also frequently mentioned when I asked women about their roles in their church fellowships. Mothers also talked about the guilt of not making the mark as an ideal 'natural' mother. In almost every part of life we can feel ourselves hampered by the guilt of not being what we 'should be'. For Clockwork mummies the guilt can become overwhelming and it is for this reason that I have chosen to put it in this chapter.

Why Do We Feel Guilty?

Does an overwhelming feeling of guilt felt by a mother in paid employment imply that she has made a wrong choice? Would she feel less guilty at home? Probably not. The guilt trap is often described as being a choice between feeling guilty for being separated from the kids while you shore up the family's income or feeling guilty for staying at home and depleting the income without making any contribution.

I hope you realise from what's already been said in this chapter that being in paid employment is not automatically a wrong choice. In that case, where does all this guilt come from? It comes from the belief prevalent in our culture that there must be something 'unnatural' about you as a mother if you want to go out to work. This belief was brought into being in the earlier part of this century by psychologists and educationalists such as Freud and Piaget. The combined effect of their theories seemed to lay the blame for all adolescent misconduct and adult neuroses firmly on the mother. On one side of the coin they rightly elevated the crucial role of a mother but they also made it sound as if the worst thing a mother could do to her child was to separate herself from it, even for a few hours. Many more recent studies have drawn different conclusions. For example, it has been shown that a wider social network of grannies, fathers, siblings and, yes, even childminders, is beneficial to the child's emotional and intellectual development. Other findings show that the syndrome of an over-protective mother can be as harmful as a mother who is absent for long periods of time.

Children in child care can often be more independent and more self-confident than those at home. These conflicting theories should not make us feel that 'we just can't win'. If there is no definitive 'best' way of caring for children then it simply means that the responsibility lies with us as individual parents to know our own children and rightly assess their needs and capacity for social interaction. It is down to us to balance how much time we feel it is acceptable for us to be 'at work' and for our children to be cared for by someone else. The identity of that 'someone' obviously influences our decision; fathers and grandmothers may be available and suitable care-givers for some families but may be unavailable or unsuitable for others.

Babies and small children have been shown to benefit from the consistent care of a single care-giver in a one-to-one relationship. The opportunity to be that one-to-one care-giver is one that many Christian women are happy to embrace. They see it as a season in their life not to be missed. In fact it may be easier for someone to make this self-giving sacrifice if they do know that their value and worth is in their relationship to God and not measured by their pay-packet or productivity.

This does not mean that women who do not choose to do this are wrong. There are a variety of creative solutions to the problem of keeping the family solvent and both husband and wife meaningfully involved with life. A friend of mine has just returned to work full-time because she can earn more in a more secure job than can her husband. Opting for part-time work has suited his personality and met their child care needs.

As children get older, the percentage of mothers in paid employment rises steeply. It is heartening to note that the older children of working mothers tend to have a higher respect for the competence of women and higher ambitions for themselves.

As Christians we know we should not be driven by ambition or greed. We know that God does not measure success in the same way that the world does. This is why we are so often coy and ambivalent about mothers in paid employment. We feel that maybe it would be somehow more 'godly' to accept a lower standard of living (even if this means living near the poverty line). I don't hold with that view. In the survey I conducted, women's earnings paid for holidays and other 'extras' like food and clothes, which I consider to be essentials. I know there are ways of living and eating cheaply and we all have to cut our cloth according to our budget, but I cannot see the point of living in penury simply to prove a point. If a woman has skills that will bring a needed income into the home, she should have no hang-ups about using them. Even if the income is not 'strictly necessary', women are still called to be faithful stewards of all their skills, not just those related to child care. It is walking this tightrope of responsible fulfilment with ambition and greed on one side and pious poverty on the other that leaves most of us wondering whether we've got it right.

Types of Guilt

There are only two types of guilt: false guilt and real guilt. False guilt is often self-induced; in essence it is the result of taking responsibility for factors that are beyond your control. Your child gets sick and has to have a few days off school. Why do you feel guilty? Only because you are torn between the needs of your child and the needs of your employer. You are not responsible for making your child sick. This is a factor that is beyond your control. Beware of making the assumption that every problem or adverse behaviour pattern in your child is automatically 'because you work'. Mothers who are not in paid employment also have children who get sick or who go through patches of difficult behaviour.

False guilt, when it is not self-induced, is put on us by the expectations of those around us. These can vary from self-righteousness condemnation from those who are not in employment to pressure from those who are! We can feel guilty whatever choice we make if we listen to the expectations of our work colleagues, our relatives or of society in general.

False guilt is destructive. It gnaws away at us, making us feel uneasy for no particular reason. It is a waste of emotional energy to allow it to linger. We have had a hard enough time coping with the crises and conflicts created by our choice to go out to work without wasting energy on needless guilt. The way to get rid of it is to know clearly why you are doing what you are doing. Praying your choices and motives through with someone who knows you well can help you reach this place of certainty. After that you simply have to put up a shield against adverse reaction. It's not that you are above criticism but rather that you are answerable to God, not to other people.

Real guilt is constructive. It is also specific. If we face up to it and deal with it through recognition of where we went wrong and repentance, then it is always a helpful emotion. Opportunities for real guilt abound in this area of life as in any other. We have to be wary of greed, of serving our needs for significance through our work, of using work as a way of avoiding difficult issues or relationships, of allowing work to become the be-all and end-all in life. These temptations are common to everyone in paid employment – male or female. The fact that they must be confronted and resisted should not deter us from making the right choice for us regarding paid employment.

Being honest with ourselves, being clear about our motivation, and realising that we do not have to explain ourselves to everyone who asks; these are the principles for handling guilt. They apply equally well to the other areas of life where guilt can hamper our effectiveness; for example in church life, 'Why aren't you on the flower rota?' and home life, 'Another "ready meal" tonight, dear?' Let us give the last word on this subject to a report entitled *Effects of Maternal Employment: A Review of Recent Research*.[3] It succinctly states all that I have been trying to say about how spinning the career plate effectively: 'Satisfied mothers – working or not – have the best adjusted children.'

Chapter 6

Rotas and Responsibilities:
The Valuable Volunteer

Have you ever considered how many of our national institutions are run almost entirely on the unpaid voluntary labour of willing individuals? If all of these people were to withdraw their services at a stroke the effect would be devastating. Many social action groups would cease to exist, charity shops would close, school governing bodies would be devoid of parental input, teachers would be deprived of classroom help, youth clubs would shut their doors, and national movements such as the Scouts and Guides would fold overnight. Volunteers provide a great deal of the care needed by the elderly and the very young. In fact, the sick, the mentally handicapped, the socially deprived or anyone disadvantaged in any way would immediately feel the effect if the voluntary care organisations were unable to function.

'Volunteerism' is an alternative career for many women. We may not place a high value on this 'career' because we have been brought up to equate status with salary, but that does not mean to say that voluntary workers are not important to society. They are immensely valuable. They are the oil in the machinery of schools, hospitals and social services. The church is another institution that would grind to a halt or slow down to a creaking state of incapacity were it not for the help given by volunteers.

In churches, volunteers can be found doing anything or everything, depending on the denomination and church structure. Frequently they run Sunday school, make the tea, clean the church, and run toddler groups. They may also play a part in the leadership and organisation of the church either as teachers or treasurers. In fact, the Bible makes it clear that if the church is to function effectively every member does have a contribution to make with their time and ability, not only their money. So the term 'voluntary work' is not quite appropriate when we are talking about the church. This is because the concept of service is not an optional one. We are called to 'serve one another in love' (Gal. 5:13). It is part of our discipleship that we should be prepared 'for works of service, so that the body of Christ may be built up' (Eph. 4:12).

The command to 'serve one another in love' comes ironically after a reminder of our freedom in Christ. As Christians we have been set free from, amongst other things, the need to work to please God or to please other people, but our freedom should not be used selfishly. This paradox which faces us is yet another balancing act between freedom on the one hand and service on the other. The purpose of this chapter is to help you keep your balance.

I grew up in a church where everyone who did anything did so in their own time for no pay. There were no paid members of staff. While this gave a strong sense of team amongst all the members, it also led to a few very weary individuals who were doing three or four things at once and ending up not doing any of them very effectively. Paul, in his first letter to the Corinthian church, makes out a sound case for paying people who are chosen by the congregation to serve them in a particular way. The 'paid leadership' principle which has evolved into ordained leadership may have a biblical basis but it also has some disadvantages. One is that the rest of us will sit back and let the leader get on with it. Another is that it leads towards a two-tier type of Christianity where some people are seen as more committed than others, perhaps even more valuable than others. The term 'full-time Christian worker' is unhelpful in this respect because we are all full-time Christian workers whatever the work is that we are called to do – manual work, teaching, being a mum or working in a shop. Whatever else we are, we are all full-time Christians, and this should be reflected in the way we do what we do.

The well-known analogy of the church being a body makes it clear that we each have a part to play if our local fellowship is to function effectively. For a body to work, every part has to be firmly attached and in good working order! While it is true that the whole of our lives is a sphere for service, most of us also acknowledge that we each have a specific part to play in our Christian fellowship. The concept of 'every member ministry' has received widespread acceptance in recent years, but in spite of all these positive attitudes the whole area of commitment to 'voluntary' tasks is often very fraught. Voluntary work in a church, more so than in a school or hospital, is complicated by the words 'expectation' and 'obligation'. In the wider world people generally take up voluntary tasks because they genuinely want to; but in the church 'voluntary' can feel like 'obligatory' when pressure is applied or the guilt piled on.

In the questionnaire that formed the basis of this book I asked women, 'Would you like to increase or decrease the amount you do for your church?' One reply summed up this sense of obligation in a nutshell: 'I ought to increase it. I would like to decrease it.' We all know that familiar sinking feeling of being approached by someone at church, that certain someone who hardly ever speaks to us unless something needs doing. While they are still at ten yards and closing we are doing mental gymnastics trying to get ourselves into an unassailable position, 'I don't have time', 'I don't feel called', 'I'm doing too much already'. We know all of these are valid and reasonable things to say, so why are we left feeling such a heel for saying 'no'? (if we have, in fact, succeeded in saying 'no'). Most of us know we do want to play an effective part in church life but deciding what that part should be can often be like walking through a minefield where other people's expectations can explode in our faces. We also have to be careful not to fall down the yawning chasm of 'need'. If we tumble into it we will find ourselves up to our knees in resentment. A need expressed is not necessarily a personal call to service, but because it is so easy to feel obliged we can find ourselves taking on a task for which we are totally unsuited.

Nor is it easy for those who have to find volunteers. There is a very great temptation to accept the first warm and willing person who offers their services. So the church can end up looking like an empty field with a few very busy individuals digging themselves deeper and deeper into the pitfalls of need, rather than an effective team of harvesters getting on with bringing in the sheaves.

Out of all my correspondents, 91 per cent said they did voluntary tasks in the churches or fellowships. Most did three or four tasks. Thirty-nine per cent did some form of voluntary work in their community. This means that a considerable number do both. Of all those who had church responsibilities, 16 per cent admitted that what they did was not related to their personality or gifts. The most common reasons they gave for staying in a post were 'needs must', 'there's no-one else to do it'. I'm glad that this percentage is so reassuringly low and I hope that it is representative of the wider Christian community because there are few more uncomfortable positions than having to put your time and energy into a task for which you feel unsuited or ill-equipped. Fear of putting yourself in such a position puts many people off the idea of offering themselves in the first place. Others have offered and served but feel their good will was abused or overlooked. They were left feeling 'landed on' and this feeling led them to resentment and eventually disillusionment, making it all the more unlikely that they will volunteer the next time.

So how can we know how to choose wisely in order to be sure that we end up doing something within our capabilities which fits with our lifestyle? If we are not going to end up frustrated or disillusioned, we need to be clear about what are the wrong motives for 'ministry' and what are the right ones. Once we know why we are serving, then we are better placed to work out how we should serve.

Wrong Motives for Ministry

As I've already said, the 'needs must' approach to Christian service whereby you take on jobs just because you feel obliged to, or because there are few others around who are competent to do so, is an unhelpful motive for ministry. You will end up resenting not only the time spent on the task but also anyone else who doesn't appear to be pulling their weight in quite the same way as you are.

Obligation is not the only inadequate motive for voluntary work. There are several others. Frustration is one. You can hear frustration in the attitude that says, 'What this place needs is a good shake-up' or 'What this place needs is a someone to lead properly.' I'm not making out a case for ineffective leadership. People gifted in leadership should be able to lead, but those who aspire to leadership need to beware of their own 'need to run the show'. Someone complaining that 'things are not being done properly' often really means, 'Things are not being done the way I'd like them to be done.' Frustration is a poor motive for ministry, because serving God and serving others is often a frustrating enough business anyway, so if we embark on a mission to set the world to rights by making everyone else see things the way we do or do things the way we do we will only end up disappointed. World domination is not a worthy goal even if it is only our own small world we seek to dominate.

Frustration is often born out of our external circumstances but several other motives come from our internal drives. Several of my correspondents admitted to 'serving out of a need to prove I can cope' or 'serving in order to demonstrate competence'. The problem with this motive is that it only sustains us when the thing we are doing is deemed to be 'successful'. Failure isn't allowed. If we fail we reckon our whole effort to have been wasted and are less likely to try again. Genuine service motivated by love will persevere through failure or unfruitful times. We don't serve God on the condition that he'll make our work successful. Even when we are serving in the right area with the right motivation the harvest may be a long time coming (Gal. 6:9).

Closely related to the need to demonstrate competence is the desire to please others and win approval. This is such a basic human motive it's hard for any of us to honestly say we are not influenced by it. In one sense of course it is right to live and work in a way that meets with the approval of others. Jesus himself said, 'Let your light shine before men, that they may see your good deeds and praise your Father in heaven' (Matt. 5:16). The tricky bit is that final phrase. Our service is meant to cause others to praise God. Most of us would quite like them to praise us at the same time!

Jesus describes a servant at the end of a hard day's labour saying 'We are unworthy servants; we have only done our duty' (Luke 17:10). Most of us find these words rather hard to swallow because we live in a culture where duty is an alien concept. We hear far more about people's rights than we do about their duties. So we come into the church, take up a task and feel that somehow we have done God a favour and that he owes us something as a result; or if he doesn't, other people do. Whereas the opposite is true. Service is a privilege, not a 'grace and favour' we do for God; and he does not owe us anything, we owe him everything.

It really does hurt when we feel we have pulled out all the stops for other people, we've gone the extra mile, given ourselves in self-sacrificial service and no-one has noticed. Of course in a perfect church someone would have noticed and encouraged us, but the church is still a long way off that state of perfection so if your only motivation is to gain the approval of others or hear a warm round of applause, you will again be quickly disappointed.

So many Christians have become aware of this minefield

of mixed motives that they have withdrawn altogether. If their gift is leadership they don't want to be misunderstood as being self-promoting. Others have felt unappreciated, unsupported or at odds with the direction in which the church seems to be going. In such circumstances it is easier to stand on the sidelines and criticise than to get stuck in and work through the difficulties.

I've already described the church being like a group of workers in a harvest field, but it is also like a team on a football field. This football field has no spectator stands. You are either in the game or you are not. There may be a few paid positions, such as the manager and trainer who don't do much running up and down after the ball, but apart from them the success of the game depends on every team member playing their part. Victory is only gained when we go out together to face the opposition and score goals. Training sessions and team huddles may be vital but whatever else we are doing at these type of events, we are not playing football.

Sometimes we forget that church is meant to be a team game. When Paul describes the church he says *we* as in '*We* are God's workmanship, created in Christ Jesus to do good works, which God prepared in advance for us to do' (Eph. 2:10). The plural in this verse is clear but in many other verses our language lets us down by failing to make it clear that most of the time, it is 'you' plural, not 'you' singular. This could leave us with a highly individualistic view of the Christian life, whereas our faith is meant to be a corporate demonstration of Christ to the world in his body, the Church; not a display of enterprising acts performed by impressive individuals.

So, assuming we do want to be part of this corporate expression of faith in the world, how do we sort out what we are meant to be doing? The way to get to the heart of the matter as far as motives are concerned is to ask yourself the following question: 'Who am I serving?' The answer is usually one of two possibilities: either you are serving God or you are serving yourself. 'Self-service' motives are the ones characterised by frustration or coloured by the need for approval. A 'God-serving' motive can only have one source and that is love. When we have received and understood God's love for us then we can be freed from self-service, to love God by loving and serving those around us.

This is why service is a form of worship (Rom. 12:1). We have to be empty of ourselves in order to serve but, 'To be full of ourselves is to be blind to the glory and love of God and to the true meaning of life itself.'[1] We can only serve well when we acknowledge and reject our selfish desires and motives. Empty of these and empty of our own resources we are more easily filled with God's resources, his love and his Holy Spirit. Running on our own drives and motivation means we will quickly run down. Only if we run with God's resources will we last the course.

Knowing What To Do

Does all this emptying of ourselves mean we should not take up a position for which our talent or gift is required? What about our personal preferences and personality? Should we ignore these as well? Clearly that would not be a wise thing to do. The way to serve effectively is to know ourselves well and serve in a way that corresponds with the kind of person God made us to be. If you are a shy, retiring type, gifted in administration, then it is probably inappropriate for you to offer to speak at the next evangelistic event (you'll be relieved to hear!). But you could offer to organise the sale of tickets, the hire of the venue or simply put out the chairs.

If you are gifted at relating to children then it makes sense not to sign up for the choir. Discerning your area of giftedness is not the only thing to be done. It is also helpful to make a wise assessment of your personality – are you a structured or unstructured person? Do you like to work with people on team or do you prefer to work alone at a task? Finally, what are you passionate about? Is there a certain group of people for whom you feel a very strong sense of empathy? Or is there a cause that really fires you up? The best place for you to serve in the church is in the place where these three coincide: your passion, your spiritual gift and your personality.[2]

Balancing Priorities

There is one other set of factors you need to consider when you are trying to decide how to serve and these are your personal circumstances. If you are a lone parent or your partner is not a Christian, it may be that your opportunities to serve will have to be limited. Even if you are married and your husband is also a Christian you must still prioritise wisely.

The single most common problem experienced by my correspondents in this area of their lives was 'resentment from their children and/or spouse about the evening meetings or extra stress caused by their responsibility'. The single most common suggestion they made was to 'put the family first'.

I am well aware of the danger of making our children resentful towards Christianity because of our involvement with church life, but sometimes we are so afraid of the possibility of this resentment that we use it as a reason not to serve in any capacity. I think it is important to think about what our lifestyle is demonstrating to our children. While naturally we want the best for them in life, does this mean bending to their every preference? If I stand back and do nothing 'because of my kids', I am in danger of demonstrating a self-protective indifference to the needs of the wider world. I would far rather set them an example of God's love in action through my willingness to serve.

Of course we need to listen sensitively to the actions and

reactions of our children but we should also be aware that they are listening sensitively to us. If all they 'overhear' is our resentment or criticism of others then they will not be impressed. One of my correspondents said she knew it was time to rethink her responsibilities when she became aware that she was 'being nice to everyone except the family'. This is like the story of the vicar's wife who asked her husband one Sunday, 'Shall we do things the other way round today, dear? Why don't you be miserable at church and cheerful when you come back?'

It is possible to serve in some capacity without exasperating our children or becoming resentful ourselves. Involving them in some way will go a long way towards making them realise that they are also valued members of your fellowship. As I grew up I remember being included in many small but meaningful ways. When my father was the treasurer he used to let me count all the small coins in the offering plate; when my mother invited a family for tea, we'd make something for the tea table together. More important than these small routines I was fortunate to grow up in fellowships where adults (other than my parents) talked to me and took an interest in me. I think it was these relationships that were the key in reducing any resentment I felt. Church was more like an extended family than a weekly chore.

It is of course appropriate to 'put the family first', but how do we do this whilst at the same time sending the message that God is central to our lives? We don't want to portray him as simply a hobby or sideline we enjoy on Sundays.

Communicating with our family about our commitment to God is a delicate business. I have two children and, like most children, they occasionally want to know which of them I love the best. The most common method is a subtle ploy such as, 'Whose picture do you think is the best?' although from time to time they accuse by complaint: 'He always gets a bigger piece of cake than I do.' I once heard of a younger child who complained to her mother, 'If you really loved me, you'd have had me first!' There's no answer to that! Children love rank and order, so long as they are number one in line. So, hidden behind their resentment of our involvement in church is the complaint that 'You don't really love me as much as you love God.' This is a tricky one. The best answer I have found is one a friend gave me to settle all disputes between two children competing to be the favourite. She told her children that they were like her eyes, each one was precious to her. She might also have added that each one gave her a slightly different perspective on life! I thought this was such a good answer I adapted it to explain the priorities in my life. If my children were like my eyes, vital and precious to me, then God was my heart, he is the source and sustainer of my life. Only when I live life with him at the centre can I hope to live out all the other relationships and responsibilities with any degree of success.

If God is at the centre of my life then I can be confident he will not call me to serve him in a way that sells my marriage or my children short. This isn't to say that children won't ever complain and spouses won't sometimes feel resentful but if your responsibility is reaping a consistently adverse reaction you need to go back and rethink your motivation: 'Is this a self-serving mission or have I really received a commission from the King?'

A Commission from the King

It is important for us to remember that the heart of discipleship is a daily relationship with Jesus. It is easy to get so heavily involved with 'kingdom business' that we neglect our relationship with the King. The Christian life is not all about Bible study courses, worship meetings or outreach events. It is about a daily walk with God. All our activities have to be the overflow, the expression of that relationship. They are not the relationship itself. So there are times when it is right to draw back from activities that are simply for activities sake, to withdraw from a ministry

which is draining our inner life, or to take time out to
strengthen key relationships. Any major life event (birth,
bereavement or marriage) should be a time for review of
our commitments. For those with small children, short-term
service may be all they can offer. The hardest choice of
division of priorities might come if your teenager takes up a
team sport that takes place on a Sunday. How will you
influence him if you are always miles away in church and
never there supporting from the sidelines? These are the
kinds of personal dilemmas we all have to resolve individually by coming back to that central relationship between
ourselves and Jesus and asking, 'Never mind other people's
expectations, what would *you* have me do, Lord?'

So to summarise all I've said so far: say 'no' to obligation,
expectation and manipulation. Say 'yes' to God and whatever you do, don't lose sight of the King.

Other Problems

If balancing priorities was the first problem experienced by
most women in the church then it was certainly not the only
one. Others included:

- Being typecast into traditional female roles. Several
  women complained about the lack of opportunity to teach
  and/or preach. Others admitted that hospitality and pas-
  toral work were simply not their thing. An admirable
  number of husbands did what was described as 'their
  wife's turn' in crèche because she disliked doing crèche.
  (Why should it be seen as 'her' role anyway?)
- Not being taken seriously in your own right because you
  are married to a church leader. Several women felt that
  they were not viewed as individuals with their own
  contribution to make; rather they were simply seen as
  'the vicar's wife' or 'the pastor's wife'. I have known
  several who have actually been unable to minister in a

position appropriate for their gifts, passion and personality because that would put them in a leadership position and such an appointment would seem to be an 'inside job'. Thus women who are effectively partners in their husbands' ministries often have to go unrecognised or are actively prevented from having any official role. It may be a scandal in the secular world for family members of government ministers to sit on goverment corporations but surely we shouldn't judge a church leader's spouse by the same worldly standard, especially not when her labour carries no pay? An official post is actually far better than a 'behind the scenes' influence for which she is not accountable.

- Feeling like a spare part. Many married friends without children have often told me that they feel like a spare part at church. They are no longer part of the youth scene but nor do they fit into the toddler-group community. Women in mid-life (or in paid labour) often say the same. They have left the small children scene and don't yet qualify for the Senior Citizens group, often ironically known as 'Young Wives'. It is in fact possible to feel like a spare part at any stage of life. Older women can feel like an encumbrance and women with small children can feel too exhausted to be of any use. The only answer to this is to remind yourself that we are each valuable in God's eyes, that our contribution does count and not to stand back waiting to be asked. If you are feeling sidelined, make the first move towards others in hospitality and service. You will often find that others feel as isolated as you do. Don't assume they can get along without you. 'God's family – incomplete without me', said a lovely bookmark, given to me by a friend.
- Feeling that you've got to go the extra mile to prove yourself simply because you are a woman. Some women find it hard for their contribution to be accepted for its own merit. Instead it is seen always in the context of their gender. In any fellowship uneasy about female leadership,

any outstanding achievement by a woman can set male egos on edge. Consequently such women receive either patronising encouragement, or no encouragement at all from men who don't want to risk sounding patronising! Church leadership is still largely a man's world but I love the story (fictional, I assume) about the lady Baptist minister who was taken fishing by her deacons. Some way from the shore she suddenly realised that she'd left her rod behind. Jumping out of the boat she walked on the water, collected her rod, and strolled casually back. As she climbed into the boat one of the deacons, oblivious to her unusual form of transport, was heard to mutter 'typical of a woman, always forgetting things'.[3] It helps to remember that we are serving Jesus and he had no such hang-ups about women:

Perhaps it is no wonder that the women were first at the Cradle and last at the Cross. They had never known a man like this Man – there has never been such another. A prophet and teacher who never nagged at them, never flattered or coaxed or patronised; who never made arch jokes about them, never treated them either as 'The women, God help us!' or 'The ladies, God bless them!'; who rebuked without querulousness and praised without condescension; who took their questions and arguments seriously; who never mapped out their sphere for them, never urged them to be feminine or jeered at them for being female; who had no axe to grind and no uneasy male dignity to defend; who took them as he found them and was completely unself-conscious. There is no act, no sermon, no parable in the whole Gospel that borrows its pungency from female perversity; nobody could possibly guess from the words and deeds of Jesus that there was anything 'funny' about woman's nature.[4]

Practical Suggestions

If, having assessed your area of giftedness, your passion, your personality and availability (no five-minute task) and having got your priorities in balance (it is a continuous process to keep them that way) you feel ready and able to launch yourself into your chosen responsibility, you will still find yourself faced with some practical problems. We will finish this chapter with some solutions to these problems.

- Be organised. This recommendation holds good for just about every area of life. Plate spinning is clearly not an exercise for spontaneous 'free spirits'! People who plan ahead not only achieve more but they do so with less 'hassle'. Simple things like loading the boot of the car up the night before with everything you are going to need for Sunday school the next day greatly reduces the chances of you leaving the house in a tearing rush with a headache and a bad temper because you couldn't find the sticky tape. Wednesdays are my busy morning so I have learnt that it pays to have my basket sitting by the front door on Tuesday evening, loaded up with everything I am going to need for Toddler group. If I can't actually put the items in the basket, I'll put in a list of things to add at the last minute. If I don't do this I risk a fraught breakfast with the kids and I might, unreasonably, decide that running the Toddler group or playing in the worship group or teaching in Sunday school places too much stress on the family. In fact it would be my own lack of organisation that placed stress on the family, not the responsibility.
- On Sunday mornings, leave your diary at home and don't go to church with a mental list of people you *have to* see. People can usually be phoned the day before or the day after, if you have to organise something. We go to church

to focus on God, not to focus on each other and even the after-service chat can be put to better use.

- Bear in mind that some people find the typical 'fellowship over coffee' very difficult. I confess to being one of these people. I'm not very good at superficial conversation and I prefer to converse with people one-to-one, so I feel uncomfortable whenever I find myself surrounded by a large group of people all of whom appear to be engaged in lively conversation. For a raging extrovert nothing could be more agreeable than a chat over coffee with fifty or more friends, but I have to say it doesn't appeal to all of us. I seem either to open up deep, meaningful and possibly tearful conversations that are totally unsuitable for this five-minute slot when proper listening is impossible, or I flit from one 'Hello, how are you? I'm fine' conversation to the next. If you've ever felt like me, let me offer you my sympathy and my survival policy. First, don't move! Stay seated for as long as possible and talk to whoever happens to be sitting near you. Failing that, talk to whoever comes up to you. Moving around puts you in the awkward position of trying to catch the eye of friendly faces, status people or of those people you just *have to* see. Remember that the value of the person to whom you are speaking is equal to the value of the person with whom you are trying to speak. Few things are more offensive than half-listening to someone while you've got 'half an eye' on someone else.

- Make hospitality as informal as possible. If your standards are too high the chances are you'll only rarely have people round for meals. The purpose of hospitality is to bless, not to impress. A 'bring your own grub' event such as a 'Pizza Pigout' can be miles more fun and far less hassle than a sit-down affair.

- Pace yourself. If you are involved leading 'the something' on a Sunday then that may not be the best day to invite that family of five round for lunch.

- Try to work in a team. One of my friends involved in

youth work said she and her husband were only able to help because there were at least three or four other families involved with the task who experienced the same pressures and limitations. When the work is shared, the burden is more than halved. Being part of a team reduces your sense of isolation, it stops you from overrating yourself and it keeps you going when you feel discouraged. Even if the responsibility is not a team-type thing, it is possible for the family to see themselves as part of the support team.

My husband's responsibilities at church require him to be there early and leave late. We wondered how the children would react to this. We knew we could travel separately to church so that they would not be exasperated by waiting around but we wanted them to feel involved rather than just accommodated, so we spent several weeks at 'family time' reading the story of Noah and building an ark. We considered how God called Noah *and his whole family* to build the ark and we talked about how we could each help Dad to do the job to which God had called him. It seemed to help. At least they didn't feel we'd taken the decision without consulting them. Other families I know have taken on tasks in areas where their children are involved so that the whole family can work together, either over the year in youth groups or helping to run a summer camp.

• It is important to know how and when to give up, step down or change track. 'Try to see giving something up as giving someone else the opportunity', said one correspondent. The trouble comes when it seems to be an opportunity no one wants. You still don't have to continue doing something simply because no-one else will. That is not a healthy situation for anyone and at times like that you have to remind yourself that groups do fold, activities do not go on forever and churches evolve. It is not your job single-handedly to maintain what perhaps needn't be maintained any more.

Despite the impression that this chapter may have given, a church is not a group of people all rushing round fulfilling responsibilites and running activities. At least it is not meant to be that way. It is a body of people who have a family relationship with each other. Some of us may feel immensely positive about the family idea; others, whose families are a tangled web of complex relationships, may find the idea unappealing. It is to these intimate family relationships that we now turn our attention.

Chapter 7

Rites and Reactions:
The Relationship Plate

A family is like a continuously evolving jigsaw puzzle. Each individual is a piece in life's puzzle and each piece has its place. The shape of your piece is usually determined by the shape of the piece next to you. So it is, that in the puzzle that is my family, my most common shape is the wife/mother shape, because the pieces closest to me are the husband/children shapes! But the mother shape is not my only shape. I am not only a mother, I also have a mother. My adjustment into my daughter shape can be heard whenever I pick up the phone and dial my mother's number.

My shape will change slightly depending on the nature of the relationship between me and the person to whom I am relating. I should like to think that this change is not so marked as to be a compromise of my personal integrity. It's the sort of change that occurs out of respect for the person to whom I'm speaking. If I were to speak to my employer in the same way that I speak to my six-year-old godson he would consider me rather over-familiar! And if I spoke to my godson as if he were my employer he'd be rather perplexed. These subtle changes of shape are the result of adapting the way I relate by taking into account the person to whom I am relating. My shape as a sister, for example, is slightly different from my shape as an aunt. And if your family is anything like mine, you will find yourself spoilt for choice as far as shapes are concerned. I am a wife, a mother, a niece, a daughter-in-law. I have a step-father, a sister-in-law, a brother-in-law, even a step-brother-in-law (if such a definition exists).

The shape of the part I have to play in my family is as

variable as the number of people in my family. It is for this reason that large family gatherings have earned a reputation they probably deserve. Imagine your whole extended family all in one room together and you'll probably feel a headache coming on. Your clan may, of course, be the exception, but most extended families are so diverse it is hardly surprising that there is so much scope for headaches and heartaches. When the only link between people is either by blood or by marriage then there is the possibility for huge diversity in age, income, gender, intelligence and beliefs. If you've ever had to do a seating plan for a family wedding you'll know the kind of headache I mean.

At such gatherings you often find yourself caught between differing sets of expectations. Your mother expects one thing of you, your husband another, and your children yet another. In the midst of all these expectations it is essential that you know your own true shape. Although you adapt out of respect for other people you are in fact a human being of a certain shape. You have a certain type of personality, certain preferences and beliefs and you are not meant to compromise these. You are not a mere amorphous blob whose shape is determined by the people around you.

If you do feel that your life is dictated to you by your family then perhaps the idea of the family as a web will have more meaning than the puzzle idea. A family can be like a spider's web of interconnecting relationships. This could be a positive image if you see yourself supported by this network of relationships but is more likely to feel like a negative image. Family relationships are places of sticky entanglement. It can be hard to find yourself stuck in such a web. You can feel trapped. Like a puzzle piece that's been forced into the wrong hole, you can feel uncomfortable. When so many people have a different definition of who you are, it can be hard to know who you really are and how you want to live.

Who Is Defining You?

As I've already said, I am my mother's daughter. I am also my husband's wife. I am my children's mother. All these are definitions that describe me in terms of the key relationships in my life, but do they really define me? Do they really tell you who I am?

Most of us are defined by 'rite' or 'right'; the marriage rite or our birthright. We cannot help this and, to a certain extent, it is perfectly normal and appropriate for these essential relationships to shape how we live our lives. There is one other thing that tends to define us and that is 'reaction'. Many of us allow ourselves to be defined by the way people react to us. Thus if someone reacts to me in a way that suggests that I am intelligent, responsible or caring I will probably feel flattered and do my best to live up to their expectations of my intelligent, responsible and caring nature. If they perceive me as a rebel or outspoken I may even endeavour to live up to that definition. As someone has once said (and you'll need to read this slowly),

> I am not who *I* think I am,
> I'm not who *you* think I am,
> I am who *I* think *you* think I am.[1]

Being connected to so many people who either define me by 'rite' or by 'reaction', I sometimes find myself asking, 'Will the real Sheila Bridge please stand up?'

None of us can help living in the midst of so many relationships. Few of us would seriously contemplate becoming a hermit in a mountain cave even if the idea does have some appeal on certain days. We were made to live in relationship with one another. God himself is a picture of harmonious relationships: three in one.

For most of us, relationships bring meaning and joy to our lives but they are also the means by which we can manipulate or be manipulated, apply pressure or feel pressured. They can be a source of great joy but also of great pain. So before we get down to the specific problems and practical suggestions related to our closest relationships, let's look at the principles involved in forming healthy relationships.

The Marks of a Healthy Relationship

When I was a teenager, an 'unhealthy relationship' was one which involved too much time alone with a member of the opposite sex! For our purpose this definition is far too narrow. Relationships can be unhealthy in more ways than the immoral. A better definition of an unhealthy relationship is *'a relationship in which the spiritual or personal growth of either party in the relationship is inhibited because of the relationship'*. Following this definition, it is easy to see that a healthy relationship is one that enhances the growth of the individuals involved in the relationship. We will have many superficial relationships that neither hinder nor promote our growth as people, but we have many more intimate relationships that do affect the way we live. It is to these relationships that the following principles apply.

1. A Healthy Relationship Is One in which the Two People Involved Are Independent, Not Co-Dependent.

This idea can be illustrated by supporting pillars. Imagine a structure requiring pillars to hold up the roof. The ideal situation is one in which each pillar stands independently, bearing its share of the load. I wouldn't want to stand under a roof supported by pillars that lean on each other. A co-dependent relationship is a bit like a pair of leaning pillars. Two people depend on each other, either for support or for one to dominate the other person's life. An independent relationship is one in which each pillar (person) stands or falls in its own right. Like some relationships, some pairs of pillars are called to support a structure. A husband and wife are like two pillars called to support the structure of marriage. In one sense their commitment is individual but if one or the other failed in their independent duty to support that structure, the effect would be mutually felt, the crash of the marriage.

An independent relationship is one in which each person takes full responsibility for their own behaviour. They are not continually thrown off track by the behaviour of another. If you live with a short-tempered husband you cannot help being adversely affected by his short temper, but if you are affected to such an extent that it is controlling you, then you are in a co-dependent relationship. An independent relationship is one in which I am responsible for me and you are responsible for you. It is a relationship where your decisions, behaviour and emotions are not dictated or dragged along by someone else's decisions, emotions or behaviour. Obviously in marriage there has been a mutual commitment to live in step with each other but even in this relationship the independent element must not be lost altogether, because at the end of the day each of us can only be responsible for our own actions. If we are independent people we will not make our choices nor base our behaviour on criteria such as 'How will you react or feel about me if I . . .?' If we are Christians, we will want to base our choices and determine our course of action on God's reaction. We will want to be guided by his word and live our life in a way that will 'please him in every way' (Col. 1:10).

Some may feel alarmed by this notion of independence. This is because they confuse independence with indifference or a lack of loving involvement with others. Independence is not meant to be expressed as indifference. It is merely an acknowledgment of the fact that, come judgement day, no-one else is going to be called to account for my life except me, so I have to take responsibility for it. I can be independent and yet also be lovingly and appropriately involved with the lives of others. This involvement may lead me to encourage them, even counsel and direct them at times and receive their counsel in return, but I cannot live their life for them. I'm not responsible for their choices and they are not responsible for mine. I may choose to carry their burdens for them through a time of stress, but if this assistance is truly loving I will allow them to pick up the responsibility for their own lives as soon as they are able. If I don't do this my 'help' becomes a hindrance to them. Making them feel that they 'need me' may make me feel good, but it is a loss of respect for their right to live independent of me. The self-giving choice to serve another is not to be one-sided. This brings us to the second mark of a healthy relationship.

2. *In a Healthy Relationship the Involvement is Mutual, not Manipulative.*

Perhaps during a crisis all the help, encouragement and support will flow from person A to person B. This doesn't matter so long as there is an understanding that at some future point all the help could flow the other way. If either party is only interested in giving or only interested in receiving, then that relationship is not mutual.

A trivial but amusing illustration of the difficulties that arise when two people are only interested in serving is acted out wherever two people try to go through swing doors at the same time. One opens the door and the other hesitates to go through.

'You first,' says the first person.

'No, you,' replies the second.

'No, please go ahead.'

'No, you ...'

And so on.

Neither wants to look arrogant in accepting the services of the other. The length of this exchange will depend on the eagerness of each person to appear humble. The amusing irony is that in all probability their resolve will weaken simultaneously resulting in an unseemly scrum to get through the door together.

This may seem silly but it is a small picture of the ridiculous ways we relate to one another when we are only willing to serve or only willing to be served. Here's how this works out in practice. Anne is a friend of Sally's. Sally is in need of someone to have her children after school for three days a week while she works. Anne lives nearby and had often offered to have Sally's children after school, even before Sally got her job. So Sally asks Anne if she can have her children for her after school and offers payment in cash or in returned favours. Anne feels obliged because of her previous offer, so she says 'yes'. She refuses payment of any kind, reasoning that she is available anyway and ought to serve her friend in this way in order to be 'a good witness'. She thinks she is 'giving and not counting the cost'. After a few weeks Anne finds that she is tired, harassed and resentful.

Who is at fault in this situation? At first glance it might seem to be self-centred Sally who ought to feel guilty for taking her friend's service for granted. In fact, the problem does not lie with Sally. The problem is Anne's. All Sally did was to take Anne's assent at face value. Anne, on the other hand, made an inaccurate assessment of her ability to help because she placed her own or her family's needs last. She had 'virtuously' buried her feelings of resentment which led her to deceive herself and deceive Sally. She said 'yes' when she meant 'no' and after a few weeks she quite unreasonably expects Sally to discern these hidden feelings.

Deceit and denial are not Anne's only problems. There is the more fundamental problem about why she feels the need to be perceived as a 'helper', someone who solves other people's problems. The low priority she has placed on her own needs may indicate a feeling of low self-worth. Anne has a 'doormat' approach to relationships which is certainly unhealthy. The message on her doormat reads, 'I'm nobody, my needs are not important.' This approach has an opposite number which could be described as 'the steam-roller approach'. The message on the roller reads, 'My problems are all that matter.' A 'steam-roller' is the person who relates everything and everyone to their needs or their situation. They are so bound up with their own needs they cannot see further than their own nose, far less see deeply into the situation of others. If you talk to a 'steam-roller' about a weekend you've just had away, she will lament how rarely she is able to get away. If you share a problem you have, she will have experienced a comparable problem that was almost certainly worse than yours.

'Doormats' and 'steam-rollers' are incapable of maintaining healthy relationships based on mutuality. Jesus said, 'Love your neighbour as you love yourself.' These two loves must be held in balance. The doormat person does not love themself and therefore cannot love their neighbour. The steam-roller loves only themself and has no love left over for others.

A mutual relationship is one in which both parties are prepared to give and receive. A manipulative relationship is one in which both parties say, 'Meet my needs'; either my need to be a 'doormat' or my need to be a 'steam-roller'.

3. The Final Mark of a Healthy Relationship Is Respect, the Kind of Respect that Recognises that Other People Are Different and Understands that those Differences Are Acceptable.

The human personality is infinitely complex. Some people are gregarious and lively, others are reserved and quiet. Some people follow their feelings, others are logical thinkers who always follow their heads. Some people are organised and efficient, other people are quite happy to run their lives in a casual even chaotic way. Some people have a flair for colour and shape, others have a flair for words and ideas. In the face of all this you could adopt one of two attitudes: either 'Everyone who is not like me is strange', in which case you will surround yourself with like-minded individuals who respond, think and behave in the same way that you do; or you can adopt the attitude that 'variety is what makes life interesting', and learn to respect all the different ways in which we function.

In fact, it is fairly likely that you will share many characteristics with your closest friends. It is easier to relate to and understand people who think, feel or function in the way you do. But we are called to live in a variety of relationships, many of which will be with people who are not very like us, and the only way to maintain these relationships is by respect.

I would venture to say that while respect is important in every relationship, in marriage it is absolutely vital. At least I have found it so. David and I have several characteristics in common. One of these is the fact that we both tend to be introverted rather than extroverted. Almost all our close friendships have developed slowly (it took us five years to decide to get married!). We both appreciate time on our own; we both feel drained by a constant round of people, even if those people are friends. Because we are the same in this respect neither of us considers the other to be strange or odd.

Respect really comes into its own when there is a difference between two people and there is one difference between my personality and David's that has been the source of much irritation, if not outright conflict, in the past. The difference is this: I live in a world of ideas and possibilities, David lives in a world of hard facts and certainties. So whenever we discussed the future I would float upward on the hot-air balloon of some new idea I had; and he'd come along and pop it with an 'air rifle' remark, usually along the lines of 'We can't afford it.' I'd accuse him of having no faith or no dreams, and he'd accuse me of being wildly unrealistic. This was a mutually frustrating experience until we learnt to appreciate each other. I've had to accept that my ideas do need to be grounded in reality.

I've also learnt the advantages of being married to someone for whom details like tax returns and insurance are not tedious irrelevances. For his part he has learnt to humour my tendency to explore possibilities and think laterally, and I have learnt to value the way he is rooted in reality. Privately we probably both still think that the other is a little odd but publicly we support each other. Respect has been the key to this development.

At this point you may feel that these three marks of a healthy relationship sound all very well and good but very far removed from your relationships. You may be thinking, 'You haven't met my husband or seen my relatives.' It has been rightly said, 'You can choose your friends but you have to put up with your family.' It is often family relationships that are the most unhealthy and unhelpful. Dominating parents and sibling rivalry may not be problems that you left behind in childhood. It is possible for them to still be the driving force even in adult relationships.

So what do you do if you find yourself in a relationship with someone for whom the ideas of independence, mutuality and respect have no meaning? For Christians, the Bible's advice is clear. We are called to 'live in peace with everyone' (Rom. 12:18), but only as far as it depends on us. It can be very difficult living in peace with someone who doesn't respect you, who takes you for granted, or who needs you to need them. The phrase 'as far as you are able' reminds us that we are only responsible for behaving towards others in a way that is independent, mutual and respectful. We are not responsible if they do not relate to us in that way, nor are we responsible for the discomfort that is created by our refusal to become dependent or manipulable.

It is one thing to deal successfully with a problem relationship with an elderly aunt and quite another to relate in a godly and healthy way if the difficult relationship is the one you have with your husband.

Difficulties in Marriage

Let's turn the spotlight on marriage in particular and start with the main difficulties commonly experienced by those trying to maintain a marriage. The question I put to my correspondents was, 'What is the biggest challenge you face in maintaining your relationship with your spouse?'

- Time. Sixty-five per cent of them said that lack of time was the biggest barrier to maintaining their marriage. Time wasn't the only culprit. It frequently teamed up with tiredness and exhaustion so that 'when you've got the time to be together, you haven't the energy to do anything worthwhile'. You cannot help but see the connection between this problem and the second most common problem:
- Lack of communication/poor communication. Thirty per cent of the women I questioned gave this as the most difficult area. They described it in a variety of ways: 'marital deafness', 'the fact that he cannot read my thoughts', 'a lack of understanding about the difference between men's and women's emotional needs', 'the feeling that my feelings are heard, but not listened to, while I am expected to listen and respond to a long list of his work problems'. Tit-for-tat conversations are the biggest hindrance when it comes to communication. We all have them. They are the conversations between spouses that run like this:

    'I've got so much to do this week, I don't know how I'll get through.'

    'You think *you're* busy . . . you should see my diary.'

    These exchanges leave us feeling cheated of the warm understanding we were hoping for. In a marriage where both partners are very busy, an 'everyone for themself attitude' is all too frequently adopted.
- Separateness. This took all sorts of forms: separate

interests, friends, differing outlooks and separate beliefs. This is the problem of two lives that began as interconnecting circles moving further and further apart until one day the circles become completely separate. If marriages were given post mortem certificates some of them would record cause of death as 'creeping separateness'. It doesn't always take a crisis or an infidelity to terminate a marriage. 'Creeping separateness' can be sufficient in itself or it can be the path leading to a crisis.

- Not enough personal space. In spite of the fact that too much personal space will result in separateness, this problem of the need for personal space was mentioned quite frequently in various forms. There was the resentment of 'having my life cramped by his work, his interests or his preferences'. 'Not enough time to be me', said another woman. Someone else shared that 'he resents it if I develop my own interests', and another wrote about her husband not having his own friendships and therefore being very dependent on her for company. These are the feelings of women who are not so much suffering from separateness but suffering from suffocation. As one woman put it, 'The things I want to do are not seen as being as important as the things he wants to do.' The attitude persists that men's needs are greater than women's. Possibly women collaborate with this myth by placing a low priority on their own needs.

- Sex. In the sexual dimension above all others, the myth of male need persists. Women spoke about a loss of interest in sex, a lack of motivation. They spoke about having to push past tiredness to '*meet his needs*'. Only one or two correspondents made oblique references to the difficulty of communicating their own needs and preferences in the sexual area. I got the impression that enjoying sex was all about making sure he enjoyed it. Other problems were boredom and routine.

- 'Me'. When asked, 'What's the biggest problem in this relationship?' only a few honest souls said, 'Me. I'm the biggest problem.' They mentioned their short temper, their tendency to nag, their moodiness, their reluctance to be vulnerable, their resistance to change. I mention these answers because even though the answer to the question, 'What's wrong with this relationship?' may not always be 'Me', a rigorous self-examination ought always to be our first response to a problem. Are we relating unreasonably? Are we expecting him to mind-read? Are our expectations unfair? Are we preoccupied with our needs at the expense of his? Are we denying our needs which leads to our resentment being 'buried alive'?

It's much easier when we are looking for ways to improve our marriage to look for ways in which our spouse should change, or to moan about ways in which he refuses to change and so 'What's the point of trying?' Many brides go into church on their wedding day with three words in their minds: 'aisle, altar, hymn'. These words don't just describe the service but sum up the wife's ongoing attitude. It is a hopeless attitude that gets you nowhere. The only person you can take responsibility for changing is yourself. Your husband will quickly work out if your love is only on the condition that he change. We have to love the husband we have, not the ideal image of a husband we carry in our heads. This first suggestion brings us on to the many other solutions and suggestions that were offered.

Keeping Your Marriage Full of Vitality: Practical Suggestions

● Time out or away together without the children. One evening a week either out together (but not to a church event) or in together without interruptions. This is not easy to achieve. If you go out it costs money and you have to find a baby-sitter. If you stay in, it takes an effort not to be distracted by chores or other interests. As one woman put it you have to 'lock the door, switch on the answerphone and drug the children' (she was only kidding about the last part!). If the children are asleep in the evening it helps. If they are not, it can be almost impossible to get a private conversation without going out. One of my correspondents enjoyed 'half an hour, face to face daily' with her husband as well as 'a two-hour lunch-break weekly' and 'occasional marriage seminars'. She described this routine as 'just keeping the relationship ticking over'! If that leaves you feeling that your relationship must therefore be on its last legs, don't worry, you're not the only one! Don't set unrealistic goals for spending huge chunks of time together if you know you are not going to achieve it. It will only discourage you. Be content with achieving a smaller goal.

- Share a hobby. This is a helpful suggestion if you are stuck for what to do once you have carved out time for each other. Sitting 'eyeball to eyeball' may not be very motivating but going out to enjoy something together may be much more stimulating. It may be taking some exercise together, walking or going for a swim. Or you could learn a new skill together. From my fairly diverse group of correspondents a surprisingly large number recommended ballroom dancing! Whilst it won't appeal to everyone, you can see it has all the right ingredients for a 'together activity': music, exercise, physical contact. Going out together for some purpose other than intense conversation can sometimes take the pressure off and result in a greater degree of communication.

- Sex. Remember good sex starts at the breakfast table! All-day affection makes for meaningful passion. Our sexual relationship will probably only be as good as our emotional relationship. For women the emotional relationship is nurtured by little kindnesses, compliments, surprises, being listened to and being understood. For men, knowing they are desired can make all the difference. One woman uses a coded entry in her husband's diary to remind him that it'll be worth coming home early! As for getting yourself in the mood, choosing to wear something seductive under your everyday gear can act as an all-day reminder of pleasures to come! Location can make a difference. If bed is the place where you collapse into a state of immediate unconsciousness, it's probably not the best place for a sexual encounter. Sex is not all that different from eating a meal. We can all get by on quick snacks, but we all really enjoy a good feast. A gourmet meal takes time to prepare but is always worth it.

● Personal space. Don't underestimate your own need for this. If possible get your husband to understand and support you in whatever you need to do. When my children were small and we were at home all day together, I took up running. If I'd had a trying day I'd be in my gear and putting on my running shoes the moment he stepped out of the car! It was hard for him to walk in and take over when he had just 'clocked off' from work, but he acknowledged my need to get out and 'get my head together' for twenty minutes and it paid dividends for the rest of the evening. If your husband simply cannot accept your need for restorative activities then try to do them at a time when he doesn't 'need' you. But whatever you do, don't ignore your own needs.

There were many more suggestions about how to keep your marriage going but all of them can be summed up by quoting Ed Wheat's 'Prescription for a Happy Marriage'.[2] He recommends that we love our husband/wife with the best possible love and using the word 'best' as an acronym he reminds us what that kind of love should look like:

B is for Blessing which means, 'to speak well to'. The words that you speak to your partner have a power to build up or tear down, so consider them carefully. A volley of sharp words will only lead to a defensive response or an aggressive return of attack. You can also bless by knowing when to be silent. Kind actions, appreciative remarks or compliments are also ways of blessing, as is the unseen blessing you bestow when you pray for God's favour on your partner's life.

E is for Edifying. Edifying means building the other person up. Cheering them on, being their biggest fan. Enlarge their sense of self-worth. A woman is built up by her husband's praise and spoken appreciation (all the more valuable if done publicly). A man is built up by his wife's loving responsiveness to him. We should aim to encourage and strengthen our husbands by giving them our respect and admiration. In a marriage each partner should aim to create a 'safe harbour' into which the other can retreat from the rest of the world. There are enough people out there who can make you feel criticised, deflated or undervalued. When you 'come home' into this relationship you need to feel warmly supported and loved. When your partner doesn't do this for you, it can be difficult, almost impossible, to do it for him but change has to always begin with ourselves. It's no good waiting for him to edify you, you have to edify him.

S is for Sharing. This is about keeping the two circles intersecting and not allowing separateness to creep in. Even if you don't feel you have many interests in common, focus on those you do share. David is a scientist who likes documentaries and I am an artist who loves words and stories. We will always have separate preferences when it comes to entertainment, but we both like eating, so food is often the focus of a shared activity. The sharing part of this prescription is all about maintaining a close friendship with your spouse.

T is for Touching. Before you were married I bet you couldn't keep your hands off each other. Now you may rarely touch one another apart from sex. If this is the case you are missing out on a powerful way of communicating tenderness and understanding. Cuddling at any time of day communicates closeness and also sends a valuable non-verbal message to your children. Appropriate touch creates an inner circle of intimacy within the family. Many of us do not touch because we will not, or cannot, dissociate touch from sex. Many women feel it is unfair to risk arousing their husbands when there isn't the opportunity to go any further, so yet again their behaviour is controlled by that myth of male need. What about the woman's need to be held, hugged and comforted by a simple cuddle? Touching and being touched nourishes our emotional life. Of all the suggestions given in this chapter this has to be the simplest but is often the most effective in restoring the romantic sparkle to a relationship.

I've talked about marriage being the creation of a 'safe harbour' for both husband and wife. It should be the place of calm acceptance into which we can head after a busy day's sailing out there on the choppy waters of relationships. The family unit can also be a 'safe harbour' for our children but it is up to the adults to set the tone of unconditional love. This 'safe harbour' idea is, for most of us, a goal to aim for. Few of us can say we have already achieved it. Sadly for many it has proved an impossible task and the marriage relationship has floundered and broken up. Others find themselves alone by force of circumstances, sometimes tragic. For all of these people it is even more vital that they nurture alternative relationships that restore them.

Restorative Relationships

I asked one of my friends to think about a restorative relationship in her life. It was at a time in her life when she had two small boys. Her mother did not live near to hand but was able to come for occasional visits. My friend thought for a while and said that, for her, spending time with her mother was a real tonic, it lifted her spirits. Aware that few women would have such unequivocally good feelings about their mothers, I explored this relationship a little further. What was it about the time with her mother that made her feel restored? She replied that they would go out shopping together and for a few brief hours she was allowed to forget that she was a middle-aged woman saddled with the responsibilities of a home, small children and a tight budget. 'We go into coffee shops instead of passing them,' she said, 'and Mum treats me to a cream bun. On any other day this would be so irresponsible, an expensive "waste of time and money". Then Mum will see a pretty blouse. "That's just your colour," she'll say, and insist I try it on. "It really suits you. You could do with a blouse that colour. It's such good value." Before I can think of any good reason not to buy the blouse, she's heading for the check-out, wondering out loud if I have anything to go with it. "It'll be for your birthday," she says.'

I smiled as I remembered that familiar feeling of being bought a birthday present in January when my birthday's in June. I don't bother to ask if it's for my last one or for the next one because I know full well that there'll be another gift-wrapped goodie on my birthday. I warmed to her description because my own mother is very like my friend's, but I can understand that many women do not have a restorative relationship with their mothers. They find it hard to relax and be like a child again because their independence would be undermined or abused. But in a mother-daughter relationship where you are secure and respected, it can be very releasing to relax back into childhood in the way that my friend described for me. At the very least, it is a helpful reminder of that relationship which ought to have been the most relaxing and restful relationship of all, the relationship in which you were nurtured and nourished; the relationship between you and your parents.

I am well aware that for many people childhood did not furnish them with a model for this ideal restorative relationship. They did not enjoy a relationship where they felt unconditionally accepted, a relationship where someone else took responsibility for their needs, not just their needs for the next meal or the next shoe size but their needs for encouragement and affirmation. But most of us did enjoy these things to a greater or lesser extent. Few of us were totally deprived but none of us received all that we needed. The reason for this is because the parent-child relationship is only a dim reflection of the best restorative relationship of all, that between us and our heavenly parent, God himself.

It is this one relationship that is the key to all our relationships. Even if I do not have a restorative relationship with my parents or with anyone else for that matter, I can have a restorative relationship with God. It has been said that 'You cannot know who you are until you know whose you are', and until I find my security and my self-worth to be rooted in my heavenly parent's commitment to a relationship with me, then the way I relate to everyone else will be flawed. If I approach others with my own needs for security, affirmation, respect, love, affection, uppermost in my mind then the result will be a self-centred relationship in which I seek out anyone who looks able to meet my needs. This will be a demanding, manipulative relationship. If I approach other people only concerned with their needs and reactions to me and deny the vacuum in my own heart then I will become the amorphous blob we mentioned at the start of this chapter, someone who tries to keep everybody happy all of the time.

The only way I can hope to relate in a healthy way towards others is by first having my own needs met by God in the context of the restorative relationship he desires to have with me. Once I am sure of my 'loved and precious child' shape in God's eyes, then I can love others in a way that is not self-centred. God does not unreasonably expect us to function selflessly with an empty centre. Instead he longs for us to come to him and experience the ultimate restorative relationships with him, in which he meets our needs for love and affirmation and from the overflow of this security we can reach out and relate effectively to everyone else.

The spiritual parent-child relationship is not only the starting point for all other relationships, it is also the starting point for effective plate spinning. In the final chapter we shall try to pull all the parts of our lives into a coherent whole in the context of this relationship. But first there is one last book in the library of our lives that we haven't yet opened. Typically it is the one that many of us shove to the bottom of the pile. It's the one entitled 'Personal: my needs, my desires and my hopes'.

Chapter 8

Me, Myself, I: The Personal Plate

I am thirty-three, and suddenly everyone is trying to sell me products designed to stop my hair falling out or my skin sagging down. If I'm honest I have to admit that it has been my own raised awareness of such dire possibilities that has led me to seek out these sales people.

I've taken advice on what to use on my face, how to use it and how often to use it. I've listened to talks on elastin and collagen (which I thought was something women had on their thighs, but this turns out to be cellulite, I don't want to know about this because I'm sure to have it in disaster proportions). I've also learnt about carbohydrates, 'moisture enriched oils' and 'life-enhancing supplements' (otherwise known as vitamins). I've even tried a free sample of a shampoo which contained 'chelating agents'. I thought it smelt nice but I think I was missing the point. I passed on the opportunity to purchase a whole bottle of chelating agents when I found out that I could provide five family-sized meals for the same price. If it came to a choice between biscuits and cheese for a week, albeit with the benefit of Mum's hair at 'full volume', or standard fare served up by someone with less than special hair, I knew which my family would prefer.

Seeing my disappointment, the hairdresser offered me a cheaper alternative: a bottle of 'stuff' costing the equivalent of two family-sized meals.

'It's aromatheraputic,' she explained.

I replied that as my hair did not, as far as I knew, have an independent sense of smell I couldn't see the benefit. I went back to my supermarket brand.

Often beauty products are not only ludicrously expensive, they are also marketed with outrageous claims. They have fine-sounding names that seem to promise so much, such as 'fresh start soap' that promised to revitalise me but it failed to wash away yesterday's hang-ups and anxieties. I've tried a tea bag of herbs in the bath which the makers claimed would 'bubble my troubles away'. The bubbles only lasted for five minutes. After that experience I refused to be taken in by a 'calming face pack', even though the idea of being able to fix on an instant calm exterior seemed very attractive. The best one of all, especially for plate spinners, had to be the 'time-defying foundation cream'. Perhaps I should have bought it in preference to my Filofax refill. If only a cream could really provide all the extra hours I need in each day!

Such products offer easy solutions to big problems and most of us are not so easily taken in. If we are having to make a small budget go a long way then 'luxury' goods go to the bottom of the list. Why else would I have looked at a bottle of shampoo and calculated how many meals I could provide for the equivalent? Our children's needs tend to take priority simply because size ten feet cannot be made to squeeze into a pair of size eight shoes. Where on the list of priorities do our needs come? Even assuming that we don't buy outrageously expensive products, do we have trouble justifying even moderate spending on ourselves? Placing your own needs appropriately in the family's budget is a problem most of us face.

Every year David and I sit down and work out our 'budget'. We write three lists: the first is for things we have to pay for, like the mortgage, bills, food and heating. The second list is a 'maybe' type list: maybe if we save enough we can redecorate the lounge, that sort of thing. The final list is a 'wish' list for items or projects we would follow up if the funds were available. If you were to write a similar set of lists for your household I wonder on which list you would put your needs? Your needs for clothes, haircuts, toiletries or your needs for a leisure outlet, a sport or hobby. It is an unhealthy situation if your needs feature on the wish list, but you may feel uncomfortable about placing them any higher up the pile of priorities, especially if you don't contribute to the family purse. Even though you know that you contribute in other ways that benefit the famiy, if you don't earn anything yourself, you can feel very uncomfortable spending money on your own needs.

This fact came home to me last autumn during a brief period when almost every member of the household was unwell. The children had persistent coughs, the guinea-pig had lost his hair and I had a slipped disc in my upper spine. With the benefit of hindsight, it isn't hard to see whose problem was the most severe! But in spite of the fact that I was in a great deal of pain, I still took three or four weeks deciding whether or not to pay for treatment by a recommended professional. In the meantime I forked out for several sets of cough medicines and a double figure sum at the vet's for the guinea-pig's skin condition. Only when someone pointed out that I'd just purchased 'hair restorer for guinea-pigs' in preference to 'pain relief for mothers' did I realise the foolishness of putting such a low priority on my own needs.

So when it comes to our personal needs, it seems that for many of us the first hurdle we have to overcome is being able to say, 'My needs count.' The next big hurdle is to decide, 'How much do they count?' What things really matter and how much do they matter?

There is no point in denying the ageing process. I accept that I am going to become creaky and wrinkly. But I do not accept that I should become frumpy, untidy or dowdy. Whether or not you hold back the years with face-lifts, implants or hair dye is another issue altogether and one I'd rather leave you to decide, but simply having your hair regularly styled, keeping fit and keeping your wardrobe presentable, all costs money. And it seems that the older I get the more I cost to maintain.

So how much should your needs in these areas count?

Aren't fashion and fitness rather worldly concerns unsuitable for a Christian woman? No. I think we undervalue ourselves and fail to glorify our Creator, who loves colour and style, if we don't take care of our appearance. I'm not suggesting that we become preoccupied with our appearance but nor should we ignore it.

If you flip through any women's magazine you will find that it is filled with features on the themes of beauty, diet, fashion and health. The unconscious assumption made by the editors of such magazines and their readers is this: 'What you see is what I am. I am just the sum total of my clothes and cosmetics. The only changes I can achieve are by a diet or by a workout. All I am is a body.' The Bible, of course, says that we are not just bodies, we are not a mere collection of chemicals and hormones. It tells us that we also have a personality, a will, we can make choices, in short we have a 'soul'. According to God, my outward appearance does not matter half so much as my inner demeanour, the way I conduct myself, the way I relate to others. Women's magazines acknowledge this part of our being with self-awareness tests, such as, 'Are you a jealous type?' or by carrying features on life and relationships. Very rarely do they acknowledge that not only do we have a body and soul, we also have a spirit. The spiritual dimension of our lives is often left out altogether.

So how do I hold these three parts of my life in balance: my physical needs, my emotional needs and my spiritual needs? I don't want to get any of them out of proportion but how do I decide on the right proportions? In order to answer this question I have found it helpful to think of myself as an apple. It may not be all that flattering a comparison but at least the connection between women and apples goes back to the dawn of creation! An apple has three parts: the skin, the flesh and the core. Each part is essential and each part is different.

The skin of the apple represents my outward appearance, my looks, my 'style'. These things matter in that they account for the 'first impression' that you give. But they are only skin deep. Rearrangements on the surface of our lives are a great deal easier to achieve than rearrangements in our personality. Most products sell on the basis of beguiling promises that try to make us believe that using a certain perfume or wearing a particular designer label will automatically turn us into desirable, attractive people. These are surface solutions to our deepest needs to be loved and valued. The real solutions to our problems are not so simplistic. It is certainly easier to eat half a grapefruit every morning to 'cleanse the system', but this will have no effect whatsoever on that ugly attitude I've been harbouring towards my colleague or husband. If I want to be different deep down I have to change more than my appearance and hairstyle. I have to change my character. This is the second part of the apple, its flesh.

There is an old proverb that says, 'Beauty is as beauty does' and it doesn't just mean that real beauty resides in a person's character. It also means that any internal turmoil or anxiety will eventually take its toll on our external features. The flesh of the apple represents the substance of our being, our personality, our emotions, our preferences, outlook, attitude and hopes. In short, our 'soul'. Over the last few decades there has been a growth of interest in anything to do with personal awareness. Understanding yourself, your personality, overcoming emotional blocks and raising your self-esteem have become the stock-in-trade of personality gurus. Teenagers in our state secondary schools have at least one lesson a week devoted to 'personal and social education'. Topics range from personal hygiene and drug dependency to study skills. Most of this is a step in the right direction, but not all the secular methods of self-discovery are constructive ways forward. At the very least they all recognise that you are not a mere biological blob, controlled by hormones and enzymes. You are a personal being, you have values and aspirations. You have developed ways of relating to the world that may hinder you or help you. Either way, self-awareness is the first step towards change. The realisation that we are responsible for our behaviour is the second step. The final step towards change is the one that is often beyond our grasp. This is 'having the power to change'. We might get as far as discovery (I have a bad temper); we may acknowledge our responsibility to change (I need to control my temper); but we may never be able to change because we lack the power to do so. This failure to change isn't always the result of a lack of self-discipline, or a lack of effort on our part. Real change, real transformation cannot take place in a person's life without the spiritual dynamic of grace, and this brings us to the third part of the apple, its core.

The core represents the central part of our being, the part that holds the rest together. If we are Christians then it is the spiritual relationship we have with God that functions at the core of our being. God's plan for our well-being doesn't begin at the surface and work its way through to the core. Instead it starts with the core of our being and its effects work their way out to the 'skin' of our lives, our physical appearance.

God's priority list for my well-being starts with my spiritual well-being. Once I am in the right relationship with him he describes me as his child (John 1:12). He tells me I am of infinite worth (1 Pet. 3:18) and reassures me that my life has an eternal value (John 3:16). He also gives me his Spirit to live with my spirit in my inner being and this produces all sorts of repercussions in my personality that result in my emotional well-being. Suddenly those 'changes' that I was powerless to bring about are brought about for me by his power within me. As I co-operate with him, the fruits of his presence in my inner being are seen in my personality: love, joy, peace, gentleness, compassion, self-control (Gal. 5:22–23, Col. 3:12). Finally he affirms and delights in my physical well-being. He created my body and honours it by describing it as 'the temple of the Holy Spirit' (1 Cor. 6:19). He would have me take care of it and not abuse it but at the same time he reminds me that it is like an outer tent that is 'wearing away' and that he has a new body ready for me in heaven. As far as he's concerned, outward adornment is neither here nor there; it is not the source of attractiveness. The source of genuine beauty is the presence of Jesus at the core of a person's life.

So in answer to the question, 'How much do my needs matter?' I have now described a hierarchy of needs. Your physical needs do matter, but not so much as your emotional and spiritual needs. If we really want to live peaceful, attractive and fulfilled lives we must pay attention to the core. The psalmist says of God, 'My flesh and my heart may fail, but God is ... my portion for ever' (Ps. 73:26). Beware of taking the 'r' out of 'portion'. God cannot and will not be reduced to the status of a quick fix remedy we occasionally use. Elsewhere the psalmist writes how the 'lines have fallen ... in pleasant places' (Ps. 16:6). He means boundary lines, not wrinkles, but we can be similarly content with our lot when we are freed from preoccupation about the ageing process, by having our inner longings to be loved and valued met by God.

Having opened the core of our lives to God, what responsibility towards ourselves remains with us? I have a responsibility to ensure that the gauges on my emotional and physical reserves do not read 'empty'. I can do this, not with replenishing creams but through replenishing activities. I have a responsibility to cultivate my outer life – my hobbies, relationships, intellectual development; and my inner life that is my relationship with my Maker. Unless I place this responsibility to myself sufficiently high on the family's agenda the chances are I will end up feeling crushed, frustrated and undervalued.

I asked my correspondents two questions about their personal lives: what were the replenishing activities they enjoyed? And how did they nourish and sustain their inner, spiritual life? We'll close this chapter by looking at their responses to the first question, ways to relax and recharge your emotional batteries, and take up their answers to the second question in the final chapter.

Far and away the most popular replenishing activity was reading. This has to be a heartening statistic for a writer! The next most popular activity was taking a bath. As someone who always reads in the bath, I warmly recommend the combination of these pleasures. Watching television, gardening, seeing friends, and listening to music all followed on close behind in terms of popularity. Exercising was more popular than knitting but only a little more popular than embroidery.

The purpose of all these activities as leisure pursuits is to help us relax. It may seem bizarre that we sometimes need reminding of that purpose but we can allow even creative or relaxing activities to become stressful if we approach them with a perfectionist or competitive attitude.

About a year ago I determined to get fitter and slimmer so I enrolled at a gym, convinced that the membership fee would act as an incentive to go regularly. Since having children I've appreciated exercise as a way of lifting my spirits and restoring my perspective. I've exercised to a moderate level purely as a form of relaxation. It has never made me any slimmer or fitter. Last year, when I set myself this goal, exercise ceased to be a relaxing activity. Instead I pushed myself to go to the gym three times a week and berated myself if I didn't make it. Very soon my form of 'relaxation' had become just another demand on my time and I began to resent it. I had to remind myself that I had a choice. I could opt for a slightly thicker waistline, a more relaxed approach to life and a more indulgent attitude to cream cakes. Or I could continue to push myself relentlessly for the sake of losing a few more pounds. No prizes for guessing my decision. I realise this isn't a very encouraging story for anyone trying to tackle a serious weight problem where hard work and sheer willpower are vital, but I'm simply trying to make the point that relaxing activities should not become demanding activities.

Some people are not very good at relaxing. They have to be on the go all the time. Even these people need to find a task that helps them slow down, something that switches off their racing mind. I am one of these people and I have found a number of activities that do the trick. If I'm tired, the best way to 'veg out' is to sit in front of the television. I try to record things I like that are on at inconveniently early times and then I can watch them last thing at night. I also knit but I knit 'neurotically'. I took this hobby up at a time when I felt so stressed I couldn't even bring myself to choose a pattern, let alone commit good money to buying wool. I knew I needed to do something undemanding but if I'd have bought a bag of wool it would have tortured me with guilt to leave it lying untouched for months. So I began to knit with the multi-coloured balls of wool left over from previous projects. The result, so far, is half a very brightly coloured jumper. When I'd completed about half of the front I realised I'd been using the 'wrong' needles, but it seemed somehow appropriate so I cheerfully opted to continue with them. When (if) I ever finish it I shall wear it on days when I need reminding of God's unconditional acceptance of me as I am. I am a loved child, unique. I am not perfectly put together but I can serve a purpose for my Creator even as I am.

There were almost as many other ideas for relaxing activities as there were women suggesting them. In case you are short of a few ideas here are some to be going on with;

Dressmaking, dancing, riding a bike, hat making, having the house to yourself, learning to play an instrument, learning a language, calligraphy, swimming, having your hair done, having a massage, talking over trivial things, talking on a deep level, shopping, visiting places of interest, listening to the radio, abseiling, cake decorating, sitting in total silence for fifteen minutes, watching a film, browsing around town alone, cooking, running, decorating, walking the dog.

The only conclusion that can be drawn from such a list is that we are all different. What is relaxing for one person is sheer hard work for another. Most of these activities involve us at a physical level or an emotional level. They are linked to our personality and preferences. They affect the two outer parts of our lives: the skin and the flesh of the apple, to use the earlier illustration. They do not have an obvious effect on our spiritual well-being but they have some effect because, when we do slow down and give ourselves time to think, we often find that we are in a more receptive frame of mind either to hear God speaking to our spirits or to become aware of our inner needs. If we don't have some way of slowing ourselves down we may never be able to reflect deeply enough to work out the 'why' and 'how' of who we are. You may not find such introspection appealing but it is a necessary precursor to change. If we want to change or grow as people we have to become aware of how we function now, and why we function that way.

So don't undervalue your physical and emotional well-being. The fact is that you will feel better if you eat well, exercise at least a little, dress as well as you can afford and generally take care of yourself. You will feel the effects of this care even in the core of your being, in your spiritual life. Nor will you be the only one to benefit. I don't want you to become overly anxious about your appearance but if you pay it appropriate attention your life is not the only one enhanced as a result. Most husbands enjoy having a wife who makes the best of her features and dresses attractively. If you can also be attractive in the undressed state this is usually a very appealing prospect for him. It may be rather more of a challenge for you but lingerie and low lighting work wonders!

At the time of the conversation with my hairdresser that I recalled at the start of this chapter I'll admit I was becoming a little over-anxious about my appearance. But then I found out that the overhead lights in hairdressers are actually designed to make you look bald and grey! I turned down my hairdresser's advice in favour of getting back to a more basic solution: food. Even my basic education in biology had taught me that hair is made of dead cells. So what was the point, I reasoned, of slapping expensive slop on the dead cells that I am meant to shed regularly in the normal course of events. Nutrition had to be the answer. Perhaps if I paid more attention to my diet I would produce better, fatter cells on the inside that would then die more gracefully on the outside (my biology was very basic). I set off to the library to investigate nutrition and found that there was little agreement about what was good for you. Some diets let you eat meat; others only let you eat carbohydrates but only in certain combinations; and disappointingly few recommended pizza or lasagna. The only thing on which they all seemed to agree was their enthusiastic endorsement of bran and other unappealing products such as prunes.

The disappointing results of my research reminded me of God's priority list for my well-being. He begins with my spiritual well-being. He makes me his child and tells me I am of infinite worth to him. Then he puts his Spirit within me to live in my inner being, and his presence and my co-operation produce repercussions in my personality that result in my emotional well-being. Finally he desires my physical well-being and expects me to take care of my body whilst reminding me that it is frail and temporary so I'm not to get too worked up about the saggy bits or wrinkly bits or even the balding bits . . .

Balding bits? Just a minute, I'm only thirty-three years old . . . perhaps I should buy that shampoo after all!

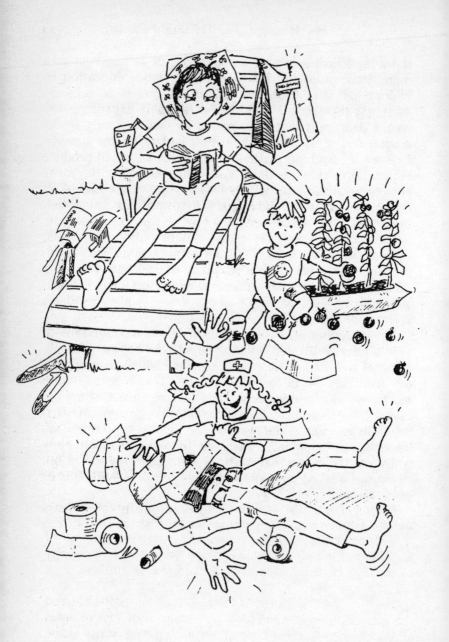

Chapter 9

Mastering the Art of Plate Spinning

You know you are going too fast when you find yourself becoming very annoyed with inanimate objects that don't co-operate.

If you've ever tried to get out of the house in a hurry you'll know the kind of thing I mean. First it will be the bunch of keys. You will fumble to find the right one and they will instantly interlock with one another, just to frustrate you. Next it will be the car seat. It will have been left in the right position for your long-legged husband and you will have to fiddle with the knob and jerk back and forwards several times, until you end up with your knees around your ears and your chin over the wheel. The final straw is always that most ticklish of modern inventions, 'the inertia reel seat belt'. These safety devices are specifically designed not to co-operate with anyone who is in a tearing hurry to make a fast getaway. The faster you tug them, the more likely they are to lock and resist your efforts. Logically you know that all you need to do is slow down but every fibre of your breathless being rebels against pulling the belt down slowly and gently.

Inanimate objects need not be the only sources of frustration. Other people can be just as maddening. Imagine a typical scene; everyone in your family is trying to get out of the house at the same time, everyone has a different priority at the top of their agenda and everyone is running to a different timetable.

Your daughter's priority is the colour of her hair-slide and she expects to be delivered to school at least five minutes earlier than she needs to be. Your husband's priority is the first task of his working day and he expects to leave the house at least half an hour before anyone else has even thought about it. Your priority is to have everyone delivered to their various places of work/education by 8.50 a.m. and still have remembered everything you needed for the day ahead. Last but not least, your son's priority is the contents of his snack box and as far as he's concerned 'sometime tomorrow' would be soon enough to leave the house for school. If these four individuals are going to successfully use one mode of transport (the car) then they have to combine and co-ordinate their conflicting timetables and priorities.

And you were wondering why getting everyone out in the morning was such hard work? Even if you do leave successfully at a mutually acceptable time, with everyone carrying their correct lunch box/briefcase/school-bag, the chances are you will pull out into traffic only to find yourself behind someone whose timetable is running twenty miles an hour slower than yours.

We all have different priorities in life. It has become fashionable lately for companies to publicise their priorities to the public in the form of some framed statement of mission. So, for example, you might find a mission statement in your dry-cleaners which politely informs you that this company exists 'to serve the public in a professional manner, cleaning clothes to a high standard'.

Whether or not we've ever written it down, each one of us carries in our heads a mission statement for our lives. We have a goal for which we are striving, we have an agenda that we are seeking to fulfil. We have a set of priorities. This unwritten agenda may not be something we have consciously worked out. It is more likely to be an agenda that has evolved as we have grown up. Typical agendas might be, 'I want to live in peace', 'I want to live comfortably', 'I want to please myself', 'I want to gain the approval of others', 'I will avoid confrontation at all costs'.

Unless you are a Christian it is probable that everything you do in life is designed to fulfil your own personal needs.

These form your unwritten mission statement. Even if you are a Christian, it is still possible that you may not have accepted all the implications of the new mission statement that Jesus gave to his followers. In John 15:4 Jesus says that the task of his followers was to: 'Remain in me, and I will remain in you'. The old catechism expresses this same idea when it describes the whole purpose of our existence as being 'to know God and enjoy him forever'.

This mission statement places our relationship with God above all the other priorities on our list. It challenges our personal agenda; it rearranges our priorities. We all know how uncomfortable it feels when 'the rest of the world' (which in most instances is your family) fails to comply with your private agenda and timetable. So we can imagine how unsettling it would be for us to allow someone else to set our agenda and dictate the timetable for our lives. And yet this is exactly what God wants to do when he comes into our lives. For those of us who aspire to be effective plate spinners, the presence of God setting his agenda may seem like a disruptive influence. We prefer to run our own lives, thank you very much. Yet if we are to live truly fulfilled and effective lives we must spin the plates of his choosing and under his direction. We are still called to be pro-active but under his direction. The focus for this final chapter is on how we can handle all the aspects of our lives under the supervision of God.

We looked in the last chapter at our own personal needs, particularly our physical and emotional needs and we are now going to focus on the needs of our inner life, our spiritual core. Don't let the word 'spiritual' put you off. 'Physical' and 'emotional' are words that we can get our heads round. They are everyday words we can understand. Somehow the word 'spiritual' with all its mystical and religious connotations is a slippery sort of word. Its precise meaning slides away from us. We find ourselves struggling to identify the spiritual part of our being. You may even doubt the existence of the spiritual within you, believing that people are solely a combination of their physical being, their mind and their personality.

The Bible teaches us that we do all have a body and a soul and a spirit. Our spirit is that part of us with which we relate to God. For the sake of simplicity, spirituality can be defined as 'how you encounter God'. Even when we all adhere to the same set of beliefs we each encounter God in our own individual way. Your spirituality may find meaningful expression in liturgy and incense or these may turn you off. Your spiritual life may, instead, revolve around modern worship songs and in relationships with others. So don't let the word 'spiritual' put you off. I hope to show you that you are in fact a spiritual being capable of a spiritual encounter with God, and that encounter may be very different from the notions you currently hold about spirituality.

If our inner spiritual core is so hard to define and lies so far beneath the surface of our lives, why bother to develop this part of our being? If our everyday lives are so taken up with the demands of family or the pressures of our job, what possible relevance does this 'inner life' have on our day-to-day routine?

Quite simply, whether we are aware of it or not, our inner core has a function in our life. It either holds us all together or it leaves us with a feeling of inner emptiness and meaninglessness. Our inner being is the place where a relationship between us and God takes place. Without that relationship we are left with an aching void that leaves us feeling that life is just a series of walk-on parts in feature films about other people's lives; we play the child, the lover, the mother, the mother-in-law and finally the grandmother. On the other hand if we do have a relationship with God, then it is this relationship that gives coherence and meaning to every other part of life. Whatever else we may be in life, we are loved by God and known to God. This assurance holds everything else in life in its place in the same way as the spokes of a wheel are held in place at the centre.

We do have many different roles and responsibilities to

fulfil in life and often our lives can feel fragmented simply because these roles are so diverse, or because we simply cannot spin as many plates as we wish and several of them lie in pieces around us.

This is where the master plate spinner comes in. He picks up the pieces, sets the pace and holds everything in balance. He is not another plate in our lives, he is far more than that. When I originally planned this book I planned for eight plates: motherhood (stages one and two), homemaker, career woman, relationships, church worker, personal life and spiritual life. I am grateful to the friend who reviewed my plan and pointed out that the 'spiritual' is more than just another plate. Spirituality is not a separate thing I 'do'. Every part of my life has a spiritual dimension. I am a spiritual being all the time in all my roles. If God is present in my life then he is present at all times. He doesn't suddenly 'turn up' when I bow my head or close my eyes to pray.

It is for this reason that the uncovering and developing of my spiritual life is the key to mastering the art of plate spinning. Successful plate spinning is not merely about good planning and self-discipline. It's much more than that. Mastering the art of plate spinning is all about knowing the Master.

Jesus, our Lord and Master, does not want us to live fragmented lives. He wants us to live whole lives that are centred on him. The psalmist prayed that God wuld give him an 'undivided heart, that I may fear your name' (Ps. 86:11). And we can ask God for the same blessing. In the midst of our busy lives where everything is a part-time occupation, we can have an 'undivided heart'. In our core, in our inner being, we can be centred on our relationship with God. It is a two-way relationship. From God to us flows the sense of who we are and how loved we are; and from us to God flows back our response in worship, not just the worship of our lips or hearts but also the worship that is the offering up of every part ('plate') of our lives to him.

Right back in Chapter 1, I described breathing as the only

thing I do full-time. No wonder the psalmist placed worship right after breathing as the second full-time occupation (Psalm 150:1). My relationship with God is full-time.

Living Life from the Core

You may have no problem believing that you have an inner spiritual core. Maybe you are reasonably well aware of your spiritual capacity to encounter God, but you still find yourself tempted to wonder if it's really possible to live life from the core. Is it really possible to walk closely enough with the Lord for this to affect every other part of your life?

Clearly God thinks it is possible and this is the part of your being that God longs to inhabit. He is, of course, concerned about your children, your career, your home and your relationships but above all else he's concerned to fill your empty inner being with his presence and his love. Listen to Paul's prayer from Ephesians 3:16:

> I pray that out of his glorious riches he may strengthen you with power through his Spirit *in your inner being* so that Christ may *dwell in your hearts* through faith.

The purpose of our inner core is to be a dwelling place for the Master. No matter what other hopes, plans, dreams or ambitions we have, none is to be more central than the development of this relationship. Our one agenda, or mission statement should be to have Jesus firmly enthroned at the centre of our lives ('Remain in me and I will remain in you'). It is only when he is 'at the helm' that every other activity takes its rightful place.

We may know this in theory but it can be a very difficult agenda to put into practice. If we were to put 'life' and all its demands on one side of a set of scales and 'faith' on the other side, it's not hard to see which side would come down heaviest.

Life is a bundle that consists of our needs, our joys, our pains, our children, our jobs, our chores, our home, our car, the pay cheque, the tax return and the grocery bill. All these things scream for our attention.

In contrast, faith can seem like a lightweight bundle of the type tied on to sticks by happy-go-lucky pantomime characters on their way to seek their fortune. It doesn't seem very practical and, sometimes, not even very relevant. If we put the contents of these bundles into two circles, we can either keep them separate as spheres that compete for our attention (see Figure 1)

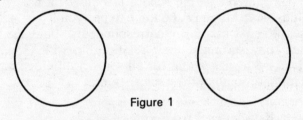

Figure 1

or we can put one inside the other (as in Figure 2)

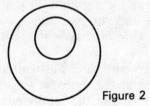

Figure 2

so that everything in the outer circle is affected by the presence of the inner circle.

It's so easy for the larger and more obvious concerns outside our lives to obliterate the quiet presence of Christ in our lives.

Our fears and problems fill the horizon until God is given no place: our worries are everywhere and God is nowhere. But he calls us to prayer: not to an escape from everything but to prayer 'in everything'. Prayer is not escapism, it is a unique kind of involvement. Our engagement with life as it does not change but as we who engage with it are changed.[1]

Prayer is one of the primary ways in which we can nourish our spiritual life and nurture our relationship with God. This is because prayer is essentially talking to God. It's tricky to have a relationship with someone if you never talk to them. But prayer takes many forms. If the only form of prayer you've encountered is the school assembly formal type or the 'God bless Mummy' bedtime type, you'll be in for a surprise. When I asked my correspondents about the ways in which they sustained their relationship with God, they came back with suggestions for all sorts of different ways to pray. Here are some of their suggestions:

- Pray with someone else. A prayer partner is someone with whom you agree to pray regularly over a period of time. You can pray for each other's daily lives, decisions, and relationships and you can pray for a change in each other's lives: the kind of change that comes with spiritual growth.
- Pray in the family, with your husband and your children, over a cup of tea in the morning or after supper in the evening. Open prayer in the family acknowledges Jesus' unseen presence in the home and answered prayer builds the faith of everyone in the household.
- Pray at any opportunity. We make an artificial divide between sacred and secular activities. Whilst it is undoubtedly good to have moments set aside when we can focus solely on God, it is also helpful to have a prayerful attitude throughout the day.
- One of the ways of cultivating an awareness of God's presence would be to play worship tapes. These can lift our spirits and the Holy Spirit can often speak to us

through them. If the words are taken from Scripture then verses and promises stay in your mind.

- Memorise Scripture. Without the help of music this may seem like hard graft but it pays big dividends as far as changing your outlook and raising your awareness of God in your life. It also helps you to feel more confident about what you believe and it's amazing how much more you get out of a short passage when you commit it to memory.
- Set aside time to spend with God, reading and or praying. Don't set yourself an unrealistic goal. If five minutes at a time is achievable then aim for just that. Find a way of reading your Bible and praying that suits you. You could read a large portion of Scripture each day using a Bible in a Year book or you could listen to shorter portions on tapes. Use some of the many notes available to help you get the most out of the passage. Some people find it helpful to light a candle; others find a certain posture or place helps them to concentrate. None of these are important in themselves, they are merely tools to aid concentration.
- If you struggle to have a regular time set aside to pray and read, don't load yourself down with guilt. People who are busy spinning all of life's plates are often the very people who do find it hard to slow down and make time for something so impractical and seemingly unproductive as a relationship with God. If you add guilt to this initial reluctance, the chances are you'll never get very far with your relationship to God. 'God understands', wrote one of my friends. 'He's not after me with a big stick.' Another wrote that 'we need to accept that we fail daily to live up to God and yet he accepts us, there should be no fear in coming to him, no recriminations'.
- Finally, look out for God's presence in unexpected moments. Several women made this suggestion and reported that they had learned to feel God's love in the laughter of their children or see beauty even in the bubbles in the sink. Not all of us have the imaginative

capacity to do this, but it is still a good discipline to slow down sufficiently in order to enjoy the simple physical pleasure of many tasks. If we are going too fast we may be eating but be totally unaware of the tastes and textures of what we are eating. We may have to walk from here to there but we are so preoccupied with what will happen when we arrive that we miss all the pleasure and rest afforded to us by the walk.

The art of living a busy life less stressfully is learning to do one thing at a time; to be totally focused on what it is you are doing at the time you are doing it, whether that is eating, bathing, talking with a child, listening to a friend. The greatest source of stress is often the build-up in our minds of all the other things we've got to do. We lose the benefit of what we are doing now because we are anxious about what we must do tomorrow. Not for nothing did Jesus tell us 'tomorrow will worry about itself' (Matt. 6:34).

In the first chapter of this book I began to explain life in terms of sailing a boat. I want to return to that analogy as we draw to a close. I have said that mastering the art of plate spinning is about knowing the Master. It is about having the Master in charge of our vessel.

Picture yourself as a small sailing boat. Your life is like a voyage. You are basically seaworthy but you are afloat on a sea of changing circumstances and your vessel is subject to all the usual pressures of tides and winds. Gerald O'Mahony has developed the idea of our moods being like tides in his excellent book *Finding the Still Point*[2] for which I was extremely grateful at a time of pressure and stress in my life. To sum up his ideas rather briefly, a fast tide is a mood that pressures you into overwork, stress, trying to do too much, trying to get everything done and needing it done at once. A slow tide is a mood that leaves you weary, lacking in energy or interest in life; you are in the doldrums with no wind in your sails. We are all familiar with these two contrasting moods and the point is that the more we are aware of their influence, the more able we are to steer accordingly. If we become aware of a slow tide we may need to push ourselves a little, or in a fast tide we will need to give ourselves some slack and take time to relax.

The tides and the winds are factors outside your control but you need to take them into account. The sails on your vessel are like your emotions; sometimes they carry you along and sometimes they are flat. Thankfully your boat is equipped with more than just sails. There is a rudder at the back which sets the direction. This can be compared to your will. You can responsibly set your will to go in a certain direction even though the pressure of tides or the buffeting of emotions fight against you. It won't be a pleasant experience, and it is no wonder that in really difficult situations it is often easier to take down your sails and simply ride out the storm in a state of numbness. Your will can keep you heading in the right direction in less serious squalls but in order to avoid capsize altogether, you must ensure your vessel has a centreboard. For those of you not familiar with nautical equipment, a centreboard in layman's terms is the 'long, thin and flat bit that sticks out of the bottom of the boat into the water'. A centreboard gives a boat stability. It may not be visible but it is nevertheless vital. It is what keeps the boat 'on an even keel'. Think of the centreboard as being your unobserved one to one relationship with the Lord. Some boats have retractable centreboards which allow for risky sailing in a stiff breeze. Those who rebel against the security and stability of a fixed board which may seem like a drag, run a greater risk of capsize. The deeper your board the greater your stability.

If you are a Christian, your boat has an anchor. The anchor is called hope.

We have this hope as an anchor for the soul, firm and secure. It enters the inner sanctuary behind the curtain where Jesus, who went before us, has entered on our behalf. (Heb. 6:19).

I once heard someone teaching on this verse and he explained that some Mediterranean ports had anchors tied to the harbour wall. The ship coming into the harbour would be 'reeled in' on this anchor. So instead of the anchor holding fast to the sea floor the idea was that the anchor was actually attached to the destination, to the harbour wall. All they had to do was hang on to the chain that was reeling them in from the open sea into the harbour. Our Christian hope is like an anchor in heaven; we are being drawn into heaven, our certain hope is of eternal life.

Some Christians may experience a time of blessing that is just like being pulled into harbour, into the safety and tranquillity of an awareness of God's love. Such experiences are great but most of us spend most of our lives sailing on the sea of circumstances, trusting in the fact of God's love and needing to keep a steady hand on the rudder. It's not all 'plain sailing', but we have the presence of Jesus on board with us and we also have the anchor tying us to shore. I love the interpretation that Eugene Peterson makes of Colossians 1:5:

> The lines of purpose in your lives never grow slack, tied as they are to your future in heaven, kept taut by hope. (*The Message*)[3]

We can only live life as it is meant to be lived, full of hope and purpose, when our life is indwelt and directed by the one who gave us life, God himself. Allowing God to be at the helm of our lives is not merely a passive assent to his authority. Rather, it is an active submission to his will as opposed to ours.

Life is not just the sum of all our activities. These are what we do. It is who we are that really counts. We are chosen, called and loved. We are valued not for all the things we do but for who we are.

It was at a women's retreat at Waverley Abbey in Surrey that Beverley Shepherd movingly described for me the intimate nature of this relationship between us and the Lord. 'It is as if he has asked you to dance with him,' she said.

> Many of us would choose to do the 'jive'. This is a dance where you only hold your partner's hand lightly at arm's length. You look very busy, your arms and legs certainly move a great deal but you and your partner stay on the spot, you do not travel in any direction. It's an exhausting dance, difficult to sustain. The Lord, on the other hand, would prefer us to waltz with him. When you waltz it is your partner's role to lead, your role is to simply follow his steps. We are to relax in his embrace and enjoy the close contact of this steady, sustainable dance. It may not look as 'busy' as the jive but the waltzing pair will travel across the floor, they have a direction.

Placing ourselves in God's arms and trusting him to lead us is exactly what we are required to do. Peterson again, this time interpreting Galatians 3:11, 12:

> The person who lives in right relationship with God does it by embracing what God arranges for him. Doing things for God is the opposite of entering into what God does for you. (*The Message*)[4]

A fulfilled and effective life is one that is lived out within the embrace of God. It does not matter whether you are a mother, or have a career, or teach in Sunday school, or however else you may define yourself. William Tyndale, who translated most of the Bible into English, before he was martyred, said,

> There is no work better than another to please God; to pour water, to wash dishes, to be a cobbler or an apostle: all is one.

You may not have been given so great a task, nor such a dangerous one as that give to Tyndale, but whatever the plates are that you are spinning in your life, may you know the steadying presence of Jesus at the centre of your being, bringing wholeness and meaning to all of your life.

Epilogue

I can honestly say I have 'lived' this book as I have written it.

When I was writing the homemaker chapter I turned the house upside down, giving it a total overhaul and partial redecoration.

When I began work on the career woman chapter I received a job offer out of the blue which lead me back to the classroom on a part-time basis for the first time in seven years.

As I wrote the church worker chapter I began the difficult process of extracting myself from a post I had held for three years, in order to free up some of my time for training in a new direction.

I was reflecting one evening on these rather interesting coincidences with my husband.

'What's the next chapter about?' he enquired.

When I told him it was the one on relationships he volunteered to leave the country for a month in preference to being overhauled or made redundant! Neither eventuality proved necessary. Without his support I would not have been able to write this book. Our computer would have 'bitten the dust' were it not for his patient helpfulness in that department. I also wish to express my gratitude to Gran who took care of the family on more than one occasion; and to Flora and Bill Young and Ruthli Mortimer for their prayerful and practical support; to Sarah Miles, Alison Farnell, Marion MacLellan and Martin Saxby for very competent proofreading and many helpful suggestions; and finally to Narina Wood, a brilliant plate spinner, who helped me collate all the research so efficiently and cheered me on so faithfully.

Notes

Introduction:

1. *Isn't She Clever* by Eveline De Jong, illustrated by Charlotte Firmin, published by André Deutsch, 1988.
2. *Daily Express* 5th January 1995.
3. *British Social Attitudes Report 1990*.
4. *Daily Express* 5th January 1995.

Chapter 4

1. This information from *Act on the Facts* compiled by Peter Brierley, published by Marc Europe, UK, 1992, backed up by the *Social Focus on Women* Report published by the Central Statistical Office, 1995.
2. From *The Unlocking* by Adrian Plass, published by The Bible Reading Fellowship, Oxford, 1994.
3. From *Faith is . . .* by Pamela Reeve, Multnomah Press, USA, 1970.

Chapter 5

1. *Social Focus on Women*, Central Statistical Office, 1995.
2. Ibid.
3. *Working Mother: A Practical Handbook*, Marianne Velmans and Sarah Litvinoff, Corgi, 1987.

Chapter 6

1. *Encounter with God*, Scripture Union Bible Reading Notes, July to September 1995, Alastair Campbell.
2. These ideas are covered in much greater detail in the very useful course, *Network*, published by and available from Willow Creek Association, P.O. Box 3188, Barrington, Illinois, 60011–3188, USA.
3. From *Frogs in Cream* compiled by Stephen Gaukroger and Nick Mercer, Scripture Union, 1990.
4. Dorothy L. Sayers, from 'Are Women Human?' in *Unpopular Opinions* published by Victor Gollancz, 1946. Permission granted from David Higham Associates.

Chapter 7

1. Unknown source.
2. Ed Wheat, *Love Life*, Marshall Pickering, 1980.

Chapter 9

1. Peter Lewis, *The Lord's Prayer*, Hodder and Stoughton, 1995.
2. Gerald O'Mahony, *Finding the Still Point*, Eagle, 1993.
3. Scripture quotations from *The Message*. Copyright © by Eugene H. Peterson 1993, 1994, 1995. Used by permission of NavPress Publishing Group.
4. Ibid.

Appendix

This is the questionnaire I used to gather the information I needed for this book. Many women reported that filling in this questionnaire was a helpful exercise in itself, for coming to terms with all the various parts of their lives. I include it as a possible alternative to the time-management exercise as a way to 'draw your own map'.

For many women the task of running their lives is similar to the circus trick of keeping half a dozen plates spinning simultaneously. This questionnaire is going to ask you to consider six areas of your life.

1. The Motherhood Plate

How old are your children?

What sex are they?

What are (or what have been) the most common daily irritants you experience in your role as a mother? (apart from the answer . . . 'My children!')

Tick as many answers as are appropriate and add your own:

☐ lack of time   ☐ untidiness

☐ disobedience   ☐ sibling squabbling

☐ your own physical/emotional state

☐ other

Have you any practical suggestions that have worked for you in this area of your life?

2. The Career Plate

Are you in paid employment?

If so, what do you do?

Full-time or part-time?

Please can you give your reasons for either being in paid employment or not (for example, personal choice, small children at home, financial necessity, seeking further qualifications, lack of opportunity, etc.)

Do you do unpaid voluntary work outside the home? (*NOT* church work, which comes under section 4). If so, what do you do?

Are you doing or have you done any further training since being a mother? If so, what?

What are/have been the most common problems caused by the 'paid employment' part of your life?

Have you any practical suggestions about how to handle this part of your life?

3. The Homemaker Plate

The role of homemaker is very varied, it covers:
☐ hospitality   ☐ shopping for food

☐ home decorating   ☐ social organiser

☐ gardening   ☐ looking after animals

☐ washing/ironing/cleaning (delete any you do not do – does anyone else do these?)

☐ handling the family's finances

☐ keeper of traditions (birthday/Christmas, etc.)

☐holiday planning

Please tick which of these you do.

What do you enjoy about being a homemaker?

Which aspects of your role as a homemaker appeal to you the least?

Do you have any practical suggestions as to how to handle these unattractive aspects of homemaking?

4. The Church Worker Plate

Do you do any voluntary work for your church/fellowship?

What do you do?

Is what you do appropriate for your personality/interests? (for example, do you do the crèche because you like children, or the flower-arranging because you are good at it?)

How much time does your responsibility take up?

Would you like to reduce or increase your church work load? Or is it about right?

What, if anything, prevents you from changing the amount you do?

What are/have been the main problems this role causes for you or your family?

Do you have any practical suggestions to offer or lessons you have learnt in this area of your life?

5. The Relationship Plate

What is your current marital status?

If you are married, what is the biggest challenge you face in maintaining your relationship with your husband? What discourages you the most?

Have you any practical suggestions to offer as to how to keep your marriage full of vitality?

If you live alone with your children, for whatever reason, what are the most crucial relationships for you in your life now? Family? Friends? Other?

What are the difficulties you face/have faced in maintaining these relationships?

Do you have any suggestions as to how you can maintain them?

6. Your Personal Life

What for you is a relaxing/restoring thing to do?

☐ gardening   ☐ writing letters

☐ reading   ☐ going out with friends

☐ watching TV   ☐ going out for a drink/meal

☐ having a bath   ☐ embroidery

☐ painting pictures   ☐ listening to music

☐ knitting   ☐ exercising

☐ other

How often do you get to do any of these things?

What are the main difficulties you face in maintaining your personal relationship with God?

Have you any suggestions as to how this relationship can be maintained in the midst of family life?

Personal Details

Please circle your age bracket: under 20, 20–25, 25–30, 30–35, 35–40, 40–45, 45–50, over 50.

The Art of Imperfect Parenting

Sheila Bridge

An outrageously honest book that looks at the
difficulties of being an effective parent in an amusing
and helpful way.

Everyday real parents experience real feelings of frustration,
irritation and anxiety about their role. The fact that they know
there must be a better way to bring up children doesn't make
them feel any better. *The Art of Imperfect Parenting* rather than
being yet another 'how to get it right' style of book, is bold enough
to recognise that all parents experience anger, guilt and worries.
It helps parents come to terms with their own negative feelings
and find hope when they know they've got it wrong.

Offering plenty of real-life, often humorous illustrations, Sheila
Bridge reveals how joy can be found in the midst of the hassle and
hard work of family life.

FOREWORD BY MAX SINCLAIR

ISBN 0 340 62134 6

The Sixty Minute Father

Rob Parsons

A best-selling book for fathers that every mother will want to read

'Being a father is not easy. There's no guarantee how our children will turn out. Yet there will come a time when each of us will look back and want to know that we have given this task our very best effort.'

The Sixty Minute Father sets goals that can help every father ensure that he doesn't miss the greatest opportunity of his life:

- Building strong relationships
- Handling time pressures
- The secret of laughter
- Setting boundaries
- The power of praise
- And much more

Full of practical advice and memorable examples, *The Sixty Minute Father* can be read in about an hour and could change your child's life for ever.

Rob Parsons, a lawyer by profession, is an international speaker on family issues.

ISBN 0 340 63040 X

A Passion for the Family

Robert Ireton

Bringing God's love into the home

Jesus wants to be Lord of every area of life – especially the family. But with all the pressures of modern living, can he really make a difference at the breakfast table and at bedtime?

A Passion for the Family is a practical and guilt-free guide to the joys and tears of being a parent – and a child – today. Full of ideas about handling relationships and setting boundaries, it tackles conflict, family fun and worship, as well as how to talk about sex and money.

For families with children of all ages, *A Passion for the Family* shows how God can come into any home.

Robert Ireton is a husband, father of four and an Anglican minister.

ISBN 0 340 64302 1